CW00557925

BUSINESS PROCESSES AND MANAGEMENT

The Perpetual Improvement as a Key to High-Performance Productivity.

Ross Pypkin

Table of Contents

INTRODUCTION

In our business world, which is universally competitive and quick-changing, better and increasingly gainful ventures are to the twenty-first century what better assembly or construction systems were to the twentieth century. In an unfortunate manner, the customary business or approach involving project management, does not deliver underlying objectives, a disturbing 70% of the time. These cleared the way, more progressively, for Kaizen and Kanban (Lean), with all the advantages they bring along. A business comprises of numerous issues, and those problems are holding back to be solved. There are huge amounts of strategies and ways to deal with these problems. However, finding a technique that can take care of the issues without giving up anything with an increase in profitability is what is somewhat difficult to accomplish.

Business ventures or projects which are of various types require organized running or management to gain its completion efficiently, accurately and on schedule. While a few procedures are basic, others are mind-boggling with all its complexities and include a lot of sub-forms. In the event that any progression is excluded, the whole task or project might be duly affected. The management of work and information process is significant. Kaizen and Kanban are one of the best strategies for dealing with the processes in any business venture. This idea is intended to give individuals a progressively effective workflow by getting all tasks involved, optimized. A productive process which is efficient, guarantees ventures or projects are completed in an effective and fast-paced manner.

Managers regularly attempt to apply advanced tools and innovations to manage problems that can be unraveled with a realistic, minimal effort approach. They have to unlearn the propensity for attempting advanced technologies to take care of regular problems. Besides, leaders must grasp kaizen and business greatness not as an instrument or procedure, but as a never-completed mainstay of their system.

From the start, the techniques of improvement that is within the philosophy of Kaizen and Kanban, seem to give an answer for some sorts of problems associated with production. As a ground-breaking and successful philosophy of improvement, Lean can forestall an intending organization failure or make an organization to become a world-class operational greatness. You, as a Lean professional, want a smoother-running office, diminished lead times, increased capacity, improved efficiency, adaptable processes, usable floor space, reduced inventory, etc. The methodologies of Kaizen and Kanban can be implemented by various organizations to cause improvements, locally or can cause Lean to change the whole culture of the business. Despite your yearnings and objectives for Lean, you and numerous organizations face another comparative circumstance: moving out of the boardroom lean and pushing toward execution.

Incorporating common sense together with practice is the main subject of this book. It is for everyone: business managers and administrators, architects, and employees. Alongside incorporating the practice of common sense, Kaizen manages the jobs of directors and the need to build up an organization involved in learning. One of the jobs of top management ought to be involved in challenging managers to attain higher goal levels and more significant standards. This way, supervisors on the first-line need to challenge employees to perform on the job, efficiently. Shockingly, numerous directors or business managers today have, since quite a while ago, stopped to assume such a job. Another issue assailing most organizations today is the inclination to put an excessive amount of emphasis on showing information while ignoring learning in groups, which is of fundamental value gotten from common sense, self-restraint, order, and economy. Great administration ought to lead the organization to gain proficiency with these qualities while accomplishing "lean administration." There are two ways to deal with critical thinking and problem-solving. The first includes innovation—applying the most recent significant and high-cost technology, for example, best in class PCs and different instruments, and contributing a lot of cash. The second uses conventional tools, agendas, and strategies that don't cost a lot of cash. This methodology is called kaizen. Kaizen includes everyone—beginning with the CEO in the business—collaborating and working together to achieve success. This book will show how kaizen can accomplish critical improvement as a fundamental structure that readies the organization for truly rewarding achievements.

The system of Kaizen and that of Kanban is tied in with moving your sleeves up, getting filthy, and making change. The genuine change goes ahead on the production area, in the upkeep shop, and in the various zones of the organization and executing the ideas of Lean. Organizations frequently stall out in unlimited patterns of planning and training, with no usage ever occurring. This book is your rule for implementation and is composed for the professional, making use of kaizen and Kanban and searching for a guideline or a tool for training that can be utilized in the work zone while upgrades occur. The execution of Kanban is a physically escalated activity, and leading Kanban business projects properly requires great experience and bearing.

While examining the concept of Kanban, we are discussing stock and making a sign framework to trigger the requirement for it. The term inventory is expansive, yet for this book, the emphasis is on the framework required between the distribution center or stockroom and the development of WIP (work in process) between work territories. In a perfect world, cell assembling ought to be fused at whatever point conceivable. In any case, cell assembling may not be plausible. This isn't generally the situation, so this book can be utilized if you won't use cell assembling and need some knowledge on the most proficient method to diminish WIP (Work in Progress) and move it through the plant. This book doesn't invest a great deal of energy on the external supply chain. This isn't to suggest that creating Kanban for

the outer side of the supply network isn't important; it is time-intensive, and it is ideal to utilize customary business books that have been composed to clarify the idea.

This book is for organizations and supply chain network professionals involved in manufacturing needing to incorporate Kanban to improve the flow of material. It is for the individuals who are prepared to prevent the transformation from materials requirement planning (MRP) push procedures to kanban pull systems and need to get it going at this point. Specifically, this book centers around parts already purchased—maneuvering them into the operation and synchronizing them to genuine utilization in the assembling or manufacturing process.

Dissimilar to MRP, which make an attempt to coordinate planning and execution, driving materials into the operation as indicated by the plan, Kanban decouples these two exercises. It enables supply network administrators to design replenishment of inventory, at that point, maneuvers stock into the operation as indicated by genuine utilization. Inventory network organizers in a Kanban and Kaizen process utilize a similar base of data as their MRP partners to build up fitting Kanban parameters for each part, i.e. an arrangement for each part. When these parameters are set up, Kanban controls the execution, activating buy requests to replenish consumption. Through an iterative procedure of arranging, altering, and executing,

Kanban and Kaizen pull methods keep stock levels synchronized with demand and supply network synchronized with real production. It isn't sufficient, however, to synchronize, because synchronizing to unpredictable interest patterns may not be plausible either for the inward activity or for suppliers. To be best, an organization must balance out the business operation or assembling activity. This requires an all-out view of the supply network, which incorporates clients, inward tasks, and suppliers. A particular procedure for making production stable (and, in this way, the supply network) will be talked about, alongside a general discussion of leveling methodology. A key achievement factor to actualizing kaizen and Kanban procedure is having clear, steady communication, with all gatherings submitting to similar systems and utilizing a similar terminology. Anybody involved in the supply network knows the traps of attempting to complete a plan of production without first having communication and organizing the procedure with suppliers.

Starting with the choice to actualize Kanban and in each stage from that point, managers involved in the supply chain assume a crucial job in conveying to suppliers what the organization expects of them and the tools and methods the suppliers need to make the change to Kanban effective. All through this book, as we investigate Kanban and Kaizen methodologies that influence the production network, there will be specific communication chances to help Supply Chain Management groups (SCM groups) in their endeavors.

The book discloses how to utilize a conventional, minimal effort to deal with the working environment—where value is included—regardless of whether that spot is the line of production, emergency clinic, government division, strip mall, air terminal, or designing firm. This isn't a book of hypothesis, yet a book of activity. Its definitive message is that regardless of how much information the reader may pick up, it is of no use if it isn't tried in everyday activities. Kaizen and Kanban give not increasingly hypothetical information, but a straightforward frame of reference which is involved in taking care of issues. For that reason, it gives numerous agendas, models, and contextual analyses.

With these two strategies close by—kaizen, Kanban and this book—you're prepared to get serious and help your work move through the framework as you learn and improve your business process further and further. You'll find out about things like classes of administration, how planning and estimation are done using Kanban, about lines and buffers and how to deal with them, and—well, you'll get familiar with a great deal of things that you'll have, to enable your group to turn a little better each day. There's more, however. You'll find out about measurements and how to utilize them to improve, and we'll show a few games and activities you can use to comprehend the standards of kaizen and Kanban and get new individuals to go along with you on the cruise. There is a little area on kaizen and Kanban pitfalls and normal criticisms, only for good measure.

CHAPTER ONE
KAIZEN AND KANBAN: AN OVERVIEW

Kaizen and Kanban are terms that are established in Japanese business and manufacturing processes, especially as it created in the last 50% of the twentieth century. You can be a manager of a production framework and continue experiencing, at the same day, a backlog. In this case, what would you do? Imagine a scenario in which your employees appeared to commit some similar little errors, again and again. The business comprises of numerous issues, and those issues are seeking for a solution. There are huge amounts of strategies and ways to deal with these. However, finding a system that can take care of the issues without giving up anything with an upgrade in profitability is the thing that difficult to accomplish.

We realize that from good implementation and utilization of Kaizen and Kanban come numerous advantages. The principle one being nonstop improvement. Utilizing the strategy of Kaizen and Kanban assists groups with working quicker and all the more proficient. Yet, more significantly, Kanban is the ideal apparatus for recognizing shrouded problems. What's more, captivating individuals in settling them by persistently attempting new, inventive approaches to make more value. Making kaizen the perspective behind the Kanban system and fueling its center standards and practices. A speedy survey of literature involving management may lead you to take a gander at receiving Kanban and Kaizen practices.

If you work in areas involving management of projects, or with project managers, at that point, "Kanban" is a word you have most likely heard previously. Possibly you even know what the Kanban approach is, yet do you know what the kaizen theory is and what the connection between the two is? The kaizen theory is the perspective behind the Kanban system and gives the center standards of Kanban. To comprehend the connection between the two, it's essential to know where kaizen originates from and what it implies.

THE KAIZEN CONCEPT

Kaizen is a concept alluding to business exercises that persistently improve all capacities and include all employees from the CEO to the mechanical production system laborers. Kaizen is the Sino-Japanese word for "development," "the act of improving terrible points." The more famous interpretation is "change for better." The steady improvement implies the progression of the advancement of productivity in any condition. What's more, the flow is from the two sides of the organization, from one individual in a little group to the most noteworthy degree worker and the other way around. It is a way of thinking based around the concept that we ought to be continually executing minor changes in our businesses, lives, and activities to improve the manner in which we get things done consistently.

Japanese organizations first executed the kaizen theory after WWII as a strategy for disposing of waste as a component of lean manufacturing. The principal Japanese organizations to apply the kaizen concept to their assembling forms grasped the possibility that to contend in the worldwide market, particularly with Western competitors, they expected to endeavor to improve at all organizational levels continually. The most prominent business to utilize the kaizen theory right up 'til the present time is Toyota.

Kaizen additionally applies to forms, for example, buying and coordination, that cross authoritative limits into the supply network. By improving institutionalized projects and processes, kaizen create means to wipe out waste.

Kaizen essentially implies change for the good. Its utilization mirrors a way of thinking that depends on endeavoring to make persistent improvement in every aspect of work activities. A key piece of upgrading change is to wipe out waste and excesses in the framework. From various perspectives embracing Kaizen is less process-oriented than actualizing Kanban. However, there are numerous covers just as dissimilarities in the two methodologies.

The kaizen procedure uses an SQC (statistically quality control) system that is thorough. This method is logical and guarantees that all principles are clung to. The system ought to be executed such that zero imperfections are experienced. This should be possible by setting up a helpful structure for the employees and workers to follow or adjust to. The kaizen procedure can enormously propel the workers and give them a feeling of self-conviction as they witness the positive result. When all is said and done, the employees ought to endeavor to proceed with the process all through by continuing the arrangement set up.

To build up your activities for progress, you don't generally need to make huge strides. The Kaizen system is tied in with doing little changes one after another. A gathering of progress specialists would be in charge. If essential, they will give improvement proposals, and the organization will adjust to those. Not at all like Kaizen, in the typical procedure and for the most part, organizations stall out in finding solutions regardless of whether they ceaselessly monitor their improvement regions. Months after month, the redundancy of this worthless endeavor gets done with no indication of progress.

Kaizen doesn't inalienably need to be a business philosophy and in actuality, can be applied to all everyday issues. The primary standard of kaizen is that everything can, and ought to be, continually improved. The kaizen reasoning has been applied to territories outside of business, for example, life-training, human services, government, and psychotherapy.

The objective of Kaizen is to remove the extraordinary eight wastes without any form of investment. Such an objective is accomplished by finding a way to expand profitability and increase the vital favorable position by ceaselessly upgrading business processes, items, and services through enhancements in costs, quality, structure, security, reaction time, and client service. In any case, Kaizen likewise accomplishes its objective by improving attitude and abilities and thumping down deterrents, which takes into consideration an incredible and genuine workgroup that looks for the common good and sense of safety.

The foundation of Kaizen's achievement is administrative responsibility. This variable has a significant, immediate and positive effect on the financial and Human Resource benefits acquired from Kaizen execution. Likewise, Human Resource improvement must be deliberately arranged so as to ensure Kaizen implementation results. Persistent improvement in the creation procedure is difficult to reach without legitimate preparation and training. Hence, Human Resource improvement has an immediate and positive effect on Kaizen's monetary advantages. In this way, organization chiefs and executives must concentrate their endeavors on preparing production operators and supervisors, since they are genuine change specialists.

The motive of kaizen

To make a superior working environment to accomplish a decent outcome.

Attention to the present situation by being available "Gemba" (The genuine spot) as an individual.

Disposal of overburdened things that are affecting your representative's work life.

Creating relationship building abilities to enhance and adjust.

Waste (pointless additional readiness to accomplish the work) decreases.

It is expanding profitability by breaking down issues up to the root.

We are gathering everybody under one Shared Vision by characterizing objectives to all the working individuals.

PRINCIPLES OF KAIZEN

Kaizen is grounded in four key principles:

- Positive constraints: It alludes to making constrains that forestall defective items generation. Examples of these constraints are: ZERO inventories, JIT conveyances, and creation stoppages because of anomalies. On one hand, both zero inventories and JIT conveyances maintain a strategic distance from the generation of low-quality items, since there are no inputs or finished items to supplant the ones that are already damaged. Hence, elimination of inventory or critical decrease is a form of constraint making items and materials to be gotten and conveyed by specifications. Then again, since production stoppages cost time and cash, organizations are compelled to find the root cause for each product defect so as to evade future production disturbances.

- Negative constraints: It represents the disposal of material sticks that slow down or hinder production.

- Focus: Every organization has restricted assets. The ideal route for enhancing assets is by apportioning them in those business activities in which the organization is progressively serious. Knowing and distinguishing shortcomings is significant for investigating whether it is smarter to isolate activities by means of redistributing and focus assets on the organization's qualities.

- Simplify: Tasks, exercises, and procedures ought to be improved through poka-yoke, Robotic Process Automation (RPA), and business process reengineering, among others.

Kaizen works under these four standards. Quality improvement can conquer imperatives and improve procedure and gear format as far as quality, profitability, and time. In like manner, quality upgrade keeps away from material jams, lessens arrangement and changeover times, and improves reengineering and forms, since assets are apportioned in those exercises and procedures that bring solid upper hands. Intensity is imperative to get by in the present globalized showcase.

BENEFITS OF KAIZEN

Despite the fact that the clearest advantage is making upgrades to the process and working all the more productively, the kaizen concept carries significantly more to the entire organization. When kaizen develops into the corporate culture, individuals begin seeing it as a perspective, a lifestyle. At the point when that occurs, kaizen will improve the organization's procedure and furthermore add to the individual improvement between quantitative and qualitative Kaizen benefits. As the work proposes, the former can be measured, and they incorporate economic advantages, efficient, decreased distances for material's dealing with, less staff, diminished holding up times and cycle durations, diminished strides in processes, and decreased stock. Factors distinguished which can likewise be recognized as Kaizen benefits incorporate Economic advantages, Competitive advantages, and Human assets benefits.

The absolute most noteworthy advantages of Kaizen include:

- Increased motivation

  Groups that effectively use kaizen in Kanban are progressively inspired to connect all the more effectively in the work and improve when they comprehend their significance in the group. Seeing their little thoughts fused in a procedure of nonstop improvement that benefits everybody, they are urged to remain connected with and contribute more.

- Growth mindset

  When Kanban and kaizen become some portion of corporate culture, and workers comprehend and acknowledge that, the business will be effective. Understanding the view and having a similar mentality and approach towards work and improvement motivates colleagues to become together with their organization.

- Acknowledgment of new ideas

The organization that endeavors to improve its procedure, is one that is additionally tolerating of new ideas. Obviously, not all thoughts will be acceptable and fruitful. However, everybody will be urged to consider new ideas and offer their issues and arrangements. A technique of consistent improvement causes groups to become acclimated to change. What's more, acknowledge that it prompts progress.

- Improved communication

Actualizing little, nonstop changes and institutionalization is simpler than rolling out major unexpected improvements. In Kanban, all colleagues are a piece of the creation and implementation of the changes. Furthermore, when the group does this together, they communicate straightforwardly on the grounds that it helps them give a valiant effort for everybody.

ECONOMIC BENEFITS OF KAIZEN

Financial advantages are results that can be evaluated. They can be estimated, and they produce benefits. The most well-known incorporate efficient, diminished separations for material's dealing with, less staff, decreased holding up times and cycle durations, diminished process steps, and decreased stock.

- Less Defective Products

  Kaizen discernibly lessens the level of damaged items in the creation lines. Recall that this concept is related with other lean assembling devices, including all out quality control (TQT), which tries to lessen waste and mishaps, therefore bringing about less damaged items.

- Unit Manufacturing Costs Reduction

  Organizations can essentially diminish item configuration times by utilizing suitable technologies and programming. Thus, models reproductions can help decrease errors in the assembling procedure.

- Request Lead Times Reduced as Close as Possible to Zero

  This advantage is the aftereffect of legitimate utilization of cutting edge business or manufacturing technologies in every office or region. AutoCAD®, for example, is a bit of programming used to rapidly create final item models.

- Expanded Work Productivity

  In financial terms, profitability envelops frameworks of logistics for materials dealings, since superfluous movements do not increase the value of the item. Right now, companies look for the basic investments conceivable in handling of materials.

- Another Kaizen advantage is sufficient usage of Human Resource aptitudes and experience, since they are frequently mistakenly sorted out. That is, employees might be answerable for undertakings that are not appropriate for them, since they either have lack of the required aptitudes and experience or can complete more jobs that are complex in nature.

- Consistence with Product Delivery Times and Quantities

This is an outcome of fruitful coordination between the nonstop improvement concept that is embraced and that of quality projects. Times for delivery are a need for Kaizen as a LM instrument.

- Material Handling

This results from appropriately sorting out the necessary materials and equipment for production. These days, cell assembling and innovation groups are productive methods for gathering a lot of exercises or a progression of machines relying upon the activities carried out, which diminishes process distances.

- Waste Reduction (Inventory, Waiting Times, Transport, and Operator's Movements)

Kaizen decreases holding up times, transport, movements, and stock that outcomes from poor human resource planning or malfunctioning machinery.

- Less Production Process Steps

This advantage is the aftereffect of the fundamental Kaizen standards, since this concept targets improving all of the production procedure steps. Such upgrades lead to end of pointless exercises that do not increase the value of the item. To accomplish this, Kaizen depends on numerous tools, including value stream mapping.

- Augmented Profits

It is the consequence of constant improvement. Benefits are increased along the supply network, yet particularly in the production lines and frameworks. At the point when organizations do away with mistakes and waste, investment funds are traduced into benefits.

- Decreased Equipment Failure

This advantage is emphatically identified with Total Productive Maintenance (TPM) forms that organizations execute in their processes of production. TPM looks to distinguish every conceivable mistake or reasons for failures in tools, techniques or hardware that may influence the flow of production.

- Expanded General Productivity

Productivity is the consequence of the rational estimation of an organization's input and outputs, which demonstrates the measure of material required to create an item. Expanded profitability infers that the organization utilizes resources that are available and accessible.

- Short Design and Operating Cycles

This is accomplished using appropriate advancements for structure and working exercises

- Improved Cash Flow

Income is improved when productivity expands reserve funds, production process waste is evacuated, and organizations have a superior presentation in new items design and procedures. This advantage is the main target of any LM instrument. Income targets producing higher profits for investors.

- Expanded and Improved Economic Stability

An organization's economic stability is the contrast between the its pay and costs. If an organization doesn't deliver anything, fixed costs will remain. In the event that an organization runs a production, variable costs will rely upon the measure of item produced. Such an item can be sold and, accordingly, benefits will show up.

COMPETITIVE BENEFITS OF KAIZEN

The best advantages of Kaizen, in a competitive manner are change in the hierarchical culture, adaptability and deftness to react to clients' requests without creating final item stock, diminished working expenses up to 40 %, waste decrease up to 80 %, expanded income, and maximum 3.4 defects parts per million (3.4 PPM) openings in the production procedure.

- The Company Has the Tools to Meet Customer Needs

  On account of a lot of strategies and exercises, Kaizen permits organizations to rapidly and correctly distinguish client needs to make an interpretation of them into item/service qualities and properties.

- New Products are more Often Introduced into the Market

  This advantage is connected directly with the innovations utilized for product structure and prototyping. Both are intelligent procedures where sales specialists distinguish client needs and communicate them to designers of products, who at that point make a 3-D or 2-D item plan.

- Improved Product Quality

  Excellent items are the consequence of activities, for example, 5S and Kanban. The former, looks to guarantee perfect and safe work spaces, with the goal that workers can quickly recognize the necessary materials. Kanban is a flagging framework for supporting the administration and materials flow, along the line of production. It takes into consideration quicker conveyance times, speeds manufacturing advances utilized all the while, and helps meet the item quality looked for.

- Client Needs are Met

  Kaizen helps address the growing and continually changing client needs, yet additionally, it bolsters appropriate asset use so as to accomplish the built up objectives and targets.

- Improved Employee Skills

  Kaizen isn't just procedure centered, since it likewise intends to improve the presentation and way of life of individuals, particularly Human Resource. In this manner, this upper hand is the aftereffect of the numerous Kaizen exercises and procedures that give instruction and training to employees. In the event that worker execution is upgraded, processes of production are thus improved.

- The Company Adopts a Systemic and Holistic Vision

  Kaizen takes into account the formation of multidisciplinary workgroups to take care of issues emerging in production frameworks. These workgroups ensure that issues are tended to from alternate points of view, accordingly meeting the interests of the entire business.

- Procedure Oriented Thinking

  Rivalry these days isn't simply mindful to the process of production, since organizations have embraced a fairly all-encompassing perspective on the supply network. Kaizen advances process-oriented speculation as an effective technique, since quality is created in the assembling procedure, and mix-ups and mishaps normally happen in the plants. Numerous LM instruments have been created because of procedure situated reasoning, including measurable procedure control and absolute gainful support.

- Improved Product Designs

This advantage is legitimately identified with the innovations utilized for the design of product and prototyping. Both are intelligent procedures where sales specialists recognize client needs and make communication to item designers, who at that point make a 3-D or 2-D structure.

- Worldwide Competition

Kaizen guarantees enhancements along the entire creation framework. Since representatives' abilities and aptitudes are accurately recognized, chiefs can without much of a stretch identify opportunity territories in HR. At the point when such zones are improved, they become an upper hand and takes into consideration early access to various globalized markets.

- Key Advantage

This advantage is the aftereffect of legitimate managerial leadership. Directors must oversee and direct the capacities and aptitudes of workers to have the option to distinguish issues and advance ceaseless improvement.

- Involvement with and Knowledge of Organizational Processes

  This is the aftereffect of compelling HR preparing projects and rewards. At the point workers are recognized for their endeavors and accomplished enhancements, they are bound to stay in the organization, which thus can hold an accomplished and gifted workforce.

- Interior Barriers Easily Removed and Authentic, and Powerful Work Teams Emerge

  This is just accomplished through shared work. Gathering individuals as a rule have a place with various regions and divisions, which takes into account tending to and handling issues from alternate points of view

- Consistent Adaptation to Sudden Market Changes

  This is particularly connected with inventory network nimbleness. Two of the most significant wellsprings of deftness are data and correspondence advances actualized in the inventory network. Essentially, organizations must focus on their creation adaptability.

HUMAN RESOURCES BENEFITS OF KAIZEN

Kaizen offers a few favorable circumstances to Human Resource: higher confidence and individual motivation, diminished client attrition and turnover of employee, improved demeanor, improved aptitudes to accomplish ceaseless improvement changes, and expanded work and consumer satisfaction. The latter are majorly influenced by the economic advantages acquired as the consequence of the organization's capacity to react to unexpected market changes.

- Expanded Customer Satisfaction

  Persistent improvement bunches must target handling production issues whose arrangements can be converted into client benefits. Notwithstanding, director's business practices should likewise be client centered.

- Expanded Employee Motivation

  A level of motivation at work relies upon numerous Kaizen exercises. Notwithstanding, the most vital variables are related with leadership and managerial duty. Business managers or leaders must give employees, particularly consistent improvement gatherings, all the vital tools and materials.

- Improved Attitude and Work Skills of Operators

  One of the most significant focal points of Kaizen is its capacity to incorporate HR in the nonstop improvement process. Since Kaizen connects with employees, they can without much of a stretch see their self-improvement, and this impacts their work disposition. In that sense, one of the most significant individual objectives for workers is the obtaining and advancement of new work aptitudes and capacities. Kaizen gives such an advantage.

- Increased Employee Self-esteem

Proficient confidence relies upon information and experience picked up after some time, at work. Henceforth, administrators need to advance a proper learning condition where employees are perceived as a significant piece of the organization, and their work abilities are profoundly valued.

- Less Cumulative Trauma Disorders (CTDs) Derived from Ergonomic Problems

Workers, particularly operators of production, care about their wellbeing and their friends'. Without a doubt, issues related with occupational hazard may cause serious mishaps or CTDs, which is the reason guaranteeing security is a top need to constant improvement groups.

- Expanded Participation

This advantage is one of the most noticeable results of effective Kaizen usage. Cooperation carries intriguing advantages to Human Resource and effects on the budgetary exhibition of organizations.

- Improved Communication Among Administrative Levels

To accomplish this advantage, organizations must guarantee fruitful reconciliation among every managerial level and look for agreement in any choice to be made, including those identified with the business' bearing.

- Positive Influence on Individuals

  With Kaizen, workers feel equipped for handling and taking care of any emerging issue. Notwithstanding, getting positive ought not be an objective selective to leaders of the improvement groups. Officials must be similarly included and committed, since the endurance of these gatherings relies upon them.

- Diminished Customer Attrition and Employee Turnover

  Since employees become exceptionally gifted in their occupations, they can effectively perceive emerging issues and understand a large portion of them all alone. These critical thinking and problem solving abilities, in this manner, become an additional worth converted into knowledge, and such information or knowledge might be lost if employees are expelled from their positions and requested to hold another with various undertakings to be learned.

- Improved Attitude and Skills of Managers and Executives to Address Continuous Improvement Changes

  Connections among individuals involved in improvements for the most part, stretch out past work to social and personal settings. These individuals in this manner collaborate outside the work place, which improves coordination in all viewpoints.

- Support and Collaboration to Build a New System

Within improvement groups, support is constantly collective and spotlights on improving not only the included region, yet the whole production and regulatory frameworks. In this manner, support and commitment from each member of the group, takes into consideration the entire framework to be improved.

Attention is Paid to the Most Important Issues

Kaizen gives workers, particularly improvement bunch individuals, the tools and abilities fundamental for recognizing the most significant opportunity zones of the organization. Dangerous occasions can, for the most part, be estimated in economic terms, by the measure of client grumblings, or by dissecting representatives' wellbeing and safety.

- Expanded Employee Responsibility and Commitment

Nonstop improvement groups are multidisciplinary in nature. In each task that is attempted, each member has his/her own duties as indicated by a work plan. These exercises must be practiced and duly reported to the leader of the group.

THE KANBAN APPROACH

Kanban is a term that truly implies visual card or sign. This framework was initially utilized as an approach to monitor mechanical production systems in a process of production. However, the term has been widened to allude to a general signaling framework that has been embraced by numerous software organizations as a piece of Agile project management. Signs are the key components of this beneficial technique began in Toyota as a way to improve its vehicle creation process. Kanban separates the assembling procedure in very much characterized phases to be effectively conveyed so as to move from one to the next, and to guarantee a quality item. As we will see, it is especially valuable in the representation of pull scheduling system, where it is utilized as a guide to keeping up ideal framework throughput.

Kanban is one of the tool to satisfy client's requests on schedule. Kanban utilized in various improvement segments, to pack the measure of work in progress as indicated by the group's ability. To begin with, Kanban tries to accomplish the ideal final item quality by compelling each stage to be appropriately executed. This evacuates disorder and immersion or bottle necks happening under ordinary conditions of production, where the most significant thing is to meet creation orders and not quality.

Kanban is one of the Lean devices intended to decrease the inactive time in a production procedure. The fundamental thought behind the Kanban framework is to convey what the procedure needs precisely when it needs it. It was initially imagined as a piece of the celebrated

Toyota Production System. It is related with the plan of pull system and the idea of conveying merchandise, just in time.

A system of pull is the place processes depend on client request. The idea is that each procedure produces every component in accordance with another department to construct a final part to the specific desire of delivery from the client. Since your creation procedure is intended to deliver just what is deliverable, your business becomes leaner because of not holding over the top stock degrees of crude, partly completed, or completed materials.

Just in time is a "pull" arrangement of production, so real requests give a sign to when an item ought to be made. Demand pull empowers a firm to deliver just what is required in the right

amount and at the right time. This implies stock levels of crude materials, parts, work in progress and completed products can be kept to a minimum. This requires a painstakingly arranged booking and resources flow through the production procedure.

Present day firms utilize modern production scheduling programming to design production for every timeframe, which incorporates requesting the right stock. Data is exchanged with suppliers and clients through an Electronic Data Interchange (EDI) to help guarantee that every detail is right.

The motive of Kanban:

It is said that improvement is endless and unending. It ought to be the obligation of those working with

Making adaptability in individuals and work culture.

A fair situation by doing one activity in turn.

Prioritization of work in the back log by the Product Owner.

You are streamlining the work procedure on an ordinary interim to stay aware of the Client's needs.

You are making the group from outside effects of progress by moving the cards in the middle of the sections.

Maximum and speedier delivery of value by making effective plans.

The Clear concentration and constant straightforwardness through the flow of product.

Handle current business state issues like - customer needs, correcting work by observing the requirements, representation of the entire procedure at once.

PRINCIPLES OF KANBAN

Start with what you are doing well now: Kanban is a strategy applied to the production lines and not a framework that discloses to you how to accomplish the work at the stations. In this way, Kanban is just a help instrument that decides whether something is being done or not.

- Accept change: The necessity for change is to improve things. Despite the fact that numerous production directors state "if something works, don't contact it," any change with Kanban, if appropriately executed, brings about improvements. Each system of production can be improved with Kanban, and that is one of the premises of a few quality concepts. Hence, organizations ought to rather say "if something doesn't work, change it" or "if something can work better, improve it." Changes with Kanban are proposed by administrators and employees, and they ought to be institutionalized. Along these lines, the job of Human Resource in Kanban is basic.

- Respect the continuous procedure, jobs, and duties of each colleague: People are specialists on what they do, they realize how to do it and when.

- Leadership at all levels: Initiative is the key. Likewise, right undertaking and management of the team, is another essential component to consider. It isn't tied in with making pyramidal frameworks but, about making every member mindful of his/her own job and appropriately do his/her activity. Besides, Kanban doesn't ensure accomplishment by itself.

- Visualize your work: Companies must recognize and track the parts and materials along the procedure and the individuals answerable for the work process. Organizations for the most part have struggles at this point. Someitmes, the work performed by a group or production process is absolutely obscure.

- Limit your work in progress (WIP): the most prescribed technique for restricting WIP is to begin a business project and have it fully culminated. Half-done tasks just expand the material flow, which includes consistent machine arrangements. In the case of something is begun, it must be finished.

- Workflow management: Limiting WIP is a piece of a lot bigger activity called workflow management. It looks to distinguish potential issues in the supply network.

- Make the standards of the procedure clear: To effectively apply a strategy, it must be completely comprehended. Right now, business leaders and employees must be comfortable with the task to be executed, including the systems for its usage. Along these lines, similarly as the 5S philosophy, Kanban targets act of standardizing work, so rules can be appropriate to everybody.

- Team improvement: Kanban achievement doesn't originate from the endeavors of a solitary individual. It is somewhat the result of improvements made by all organization representatives. Improving the workplace is a significant objective of Kanban theory, which is accomplished by upgrading collaboration abilities and improving the work states of such groups.

BENEFITS OF KANBAN

Kanban is one of the most famous advancement strategies embraced by groups today. Kanban offers a few extra points of interest to task planning and throughput for groups of various sizes.

- Planning flexibility

  A Kanban group is just centered around the work that is effectively in progress. When the group finishes a work process or a product, they pluck the following work product or process off the top of the back-log. The item owner is allowed to reprioritize work in the back-log without disturbing the group, in light of the fact that any progressions outside the present work things don't affect the group. For whatever length of time that the owner of the product keeps the most significant work things over the back-log, the improvement group is guaranteed they are conveying greatest incentive back to the business.

- Shortened time cycles

  Process duration or cycle is a key measurement for Kanban groups. Process duration is the measure of time it takes for a unit of work to go through the group's work process from the minute work starts to the minute it ships. By streamlining process duration, the group can unquestionably estimate the delivery of future work.

  Skill sets that are overlapping can lead to smaller cycle times. At the point when just a single individual holds a range of abilities, that individual turns into a bottleneck in the work process. So groups utilize fundamental practices like code survey and coaching help to spread information. Mutual abilities imply that colleagues can take on heterogeneous work, which further optimizes the cycle time. It likewise implies that if there is a reinforcement of work, the whole group can swarm on it to get the procedure streaming easily once more. For example, testing isn't just done by QA engineers. Developers contribute, as well.

In a Kanban system, it's the whole group's duty to guarantee work is moving easily through the procedure.

- Less bottlenecks

Performing various tasks reduces effectiveness or business efficiency. The more work items in trip at some random time, the more context switching, which impedes their way to completion. That is the reason a key precept of Kanban is to constrain the measure of work in progress (WIP). Work-in-progress limits feature bottlenecks and backups in the group's procedure because of absence of focus, individuals, or ranges of abilities.

- Visual measurements

One of the fundamental beliefs is a solid spotlight on persistently improving group proficiency and adequacy with each emphasis of work. The use of charts gives a visual mechanism to groups to guarantee they're proceeding to improve. At the point when the group can see information, it's simpler to spot bottlenecks all the while (and expel them). Two basic reports Kanban groups use are; control charts and cumulative flow charts. A control graph shows the process duration for each issue just as a rolling average for the group.

A cumulative flow chart shows the quantity of issues in each state. The group can, without much of a stretch, spot blockages by observing the quantity of issues increment in some random state. Issues in middle of the road states, for example, "In Progress" or "In Review" are not yet delivered to clients, and a blockage in these states can improve the probability of gigantic integration clashes when the work gets combined upstream.

- Constant Delivery

Constant integration which is the act of naturally building and testing code gradually for the duration of the day–is fundamental for quality maintenance. Presently it's an ideal opportunity to meet continuous delivery (CD). Continuous delivery is the act of discharging work to clients habitually even every day or hourly. Kanban and CD wonderfully supplement each other

on the grounds that the two methods center around just-in-time (and each in turn) delivery of significant value.

The quicker a group can convey development or innovation to the market, the more serious their item will be in the commercial center. What's more, Kanban groups center around precisely that: streamlining the progression of work out to clients

- Simplicity: Kanban gives clear and exact manual–visual control forms.

Lower cost: Production and move signals use lowcost visual apparatuses.

Agility: Pull forms react rapidly to changes in client request.

Reduced stock: Kanban limits overcapacity in forms and maintains a strategic distance from overproduction of stock, driving less "just in case" inventory.

Minimal waste: Kanban limits the losses of overproduction, superfluous stock, and going with floor space.

Improved manufacturing efficiency: Kanban keeps up control of the production line, synchronizing all process steps.

Delegation of duty: Kanban's manual–visual control forms offer obligation to administrators to make and follow up on creation and stock renewal choices.

Improved communication: with regards to a JIT situation, Kanban clarifies what administrators and managers must do. It decreases "management by shortage list" and speeding up.

Accelerated improvement: Kanban's fundamental examination forms advance and support constant improvement. ▪

Enabling JIT to work: Kanban gives two fundamental components to JIT: the capacity to oversee flow and the capacity to control stock.

RELATIONSHIP BETWEEN THE KAIZEN APPROACH AND KANBAN PROCESS

The association among kaizen and Kanban is by one way or another one of a kind. It's the obligation of the administration and workers to guarantee that they learn of the Kanban procedure too. Furnishing yourself with Kanban information will guarantee the business improves at a progressively fast rate. The procedure of consistent improvement for the Kanban framework is progressively quick and occur at a rapid rate. It causes the workers to embrace the kaizen strategy. The employees will likewise learn with time that the progress can't keep itself sustained and it's their obligation to continue pushing, in order to get positive outcomes.

Generally, Kaizen can be thought of as a model or theory of the business, while Kanban takes on a more strategically arranged methodology. One of the key likenesses in the two methodologies is their endeavor to distinguish and evacuate waste or inefficiency that is in a framework. Right now can both be viewed as 'lean' frameworks.

While Kaizen depends on an exceptionally individualized way to deal with feedback, the two frameworks do depend on a high level of internal communication. Kaizen is frequently advanced in an organization by utilizing a Kaizen board. This board looks simply like a Kanban board, yet the classes would reflect- Plan, Do, Check, Act activities.

Note that both of these practices are not totally unrelated, nor do they look to fill the entirety of the necessities of undertaking the project management processes. The two frameworks' ability to reveal and promote improvement makes each a conceivably decent force with the constant, iterative nature of most Agile advancement undertakings, and it has become regular practice that Kaizen, Kanban, or the two practices be drawn closer in organization with other Agile systems.

Since the kaizen concept is a perspective, there are different tools and techniques that can be utilized to assist you with actualizing kaizen throughout everyday life or business. The Kanban strategy is one of these techniques that is particularly attached to and go together with the kaizen theory. Kanban is a strategy of project management that was created in Japan, at Toyota indeed, during a similar time as the kaizen theory was picking up unmistakable quality in the manufacturing business.

The Kanban philosophy, or Kanban board, is a tool of project management that utilizes segments to show the different phases of work process. Cards, called Kanban cards, showing undertakings and work, are moved through the segments to show what stage they are at in the work process. The Kanban board is then used to recognize wasteful aspects, for example, bottlenecks, in work forms so as to actualize and test changes to improve effectiveness and diminish waste.

A Kanban strategy gains greatly from holding fast to the kaizen theory and utilizing a Kanban board as a tool for project management.

A Kanban board fills the double need of tracking and checking a task's progress, just as distinguishing territories for development inside an organization. As should be obvious, the Kanban procedure and Kaizen theory are legitimately associated. To lay it out plainly, the kaizen concept is the more extensive perspective behind the Kanban system, while a Kanban board is a genuine method to actualize kaizen theory in the work environment.

Despite the fact that Kaizen and Kanban both have their foundations in the car manufacturing industry, they have picked up prominence as of late in the software and technology ventures as a major aspect of Lean and Agile improvement practices. Teams who utilize lean project management strategies can profit incredibly from clinging to the concept of Kaizen and utilizing a Kanban board tool of project management.

Kaizen is a form of philosophy that everybody can apply to both their personal and work lives. At the point when a business utilizes the kaizen standard of persistent improvement, everybody benefits at all degrees of the organization. The Kanban strategy is a form of project management strategy that can be

utilized to really actualize the Kaizen theory in the working environment to distinguish wasteful aspects and improve forms after some time. In the event that you remove one thing from this reading, let it be this: little, day by day changes are the way to ceaseless improvement!

CHAPTER TWO

THE KAIZEN AND KANBAN

PHILOSOPHY

KAIZEN PHILOSOPHY

The concept of Kaizen expect that steady little upgrades can be found in each framework, and that the total of these progressing enhancements can at last lead to enormous gains in efficiency. Specifically, Kaizen will hope to dispose of any waste and excesses that is noted in the system.

There are a wide range of approaches for one to transform into a progressively productive individual or business. The vast majority of the current strategies give your business or you as an individual, certain tools to help get certain parts of your processes or life leveled out. The issue with these little efficiency strategies is that they center around little parts of your business or concerns, and not the comprehensive view. Fortunately, Kaizen theory is looking to change that standard and transform you into a general progressively profitable individual.

Kaizen is an everyday procedure, the reason for which goes past straightforward profitability improvement. It is additionally a procedure that, when done accurately, acculturates the working environment, dispenses with excessively difficult work (muri), and shows individuals how to perform experiments on their work utilizing the logical strategy and how to figure out how to spot and eliminate waste in business forms. On the whole, the procedure recommends an acculturated way to deal with laborers and to expand profitability: The thought is to sustain the organization's people as much all things considered to laud and empower investment in kaizen exercises. Fruitful execution requires "the investment of workers in the improvement." People at all degrees of an organization take part in kaizen, starting from the CEO to janitorial staff, just as external stakeholders, when pertinent.

Kaizen is most usually connected with tasks of manufacturing, as at Toyota, yet has additionally been utilized in non-manufacturing environment. The design for kaizen can be singular, proposal framework, little group, or huge group. At Toyota, it is typically a nearby improvement inside a workstation or neighborhood and includes a small gathering in improving their own workplace and efficiency. This gathering is frequently guided through the kaizen procedure by a line manager; some of the time this is the line director's key job. Kaizen on a wide, cross-departmental scale in organizations, creates complete quality administration, and liberates human endeavors through improving profitability utilizing machines and computing power.

Businesses that stick to the kaizen theory take a look at the procedures at all organizational levels and see zones that need improvements, instead of simply tolerating things as they may be, in any event, when things are running easily. They key to kaizen is that changes are not large and radical, yet rather little, at times scarcely perceptible, changes that happen after some time and when included equal improvement.

Kaizen theory underlines that changes and proposals for development must originate from all levels inside an organization, not simply from the board or leaders at senior level. In businesses that follow the Kaizen theory, all individuals from the organization are answerable for distinguishing wasteful aspects and proposing approaches to build productivity, improve effectiveness, and decrease waste.

Since kaizen was first utilized as a concept in the manufacturing business, decreasing waste is one of the most significant ways that it applies to business. If you take a gander at the achievement of the Japanese vehicle industry today, you can perceive how the kaizen theory has prompted high caliber at low costs, which is expected to some extent to the decrease of waste in the assembling procedure.

The kaizen act of diminishing waste can be applied to different sorts of waste in organizations outside of the manufacturing business. Not all organizations have similar sorts of material waste that a manufacturing plant does. However, all have waste. For instance, time is an asset that can be squandered in a wide range of organizations. The kaizen concept can be applied as a tool for time management to reduce already wasted time and improve efficiency in every aspect of business and life.

So as to accomplish the Kaizen objective of ceaseless improvement, the workplace must encourage open communication inside and over the association. A group grasping Kaizen will enable each person in the association to make recommendations, and the usage and consequences of any proposals that are received are planned to be promptly noticeable over the organization.

The procedure used to execute change follows a fundamental technique of recognizing an issue, making a recommendation for change, and afterward actualizing another system expected to improve the circumstance. This idea was additionally advanced as a major aspect of a quality control rule that utilizes a four stage approach: Plan-Do-Check-Act

The initial step includes making a plan. This arrangement will be made for divisions and organizations that explicitly need some type of progress. The arrangement should then be slowly executed until some change is seen. It's critical to consider a plan that works. Change the plan in the event that you see that there is no advancement being made. You should then take a study on the result and choose the positive.

5 Key Points of Kaizen Philosophy in Business:

Each procedure, practice, and activity can be improved.

Executes little changes after some time for consistent improvement.

Changes and enhancements originate from all levels of a business.

Everybody is answerable for identifying wasteful aspects.

Plans to continually diminish waste and increase profitability.

KANBAN PHILOSOPHY

Kanban can truly assist groups with building better products quicker and develop engineers or business men of top quality. Kanban is intended to uncover issues quick so we have a superior possibility of giving the correct item to the client in time, to keep them consummately glad. The point of Kanban isn't to lessen WIP (Work in Progress) to coordinate a group's ability and to decrease process duration as agile groups would. It is to help groups effectively spot and resolve issues that can keep them from conveying at takt time, which implies at the speed of client request – not quicker, not more slow. No compelling reason to speed up or produce more than what is essential: in lean, this is waste. Easing back down in light of the fact that the group can't keep up is not any more satisfactory than accelerating and ought to be tended to as a capacity problem. A definitive objective is to completely fulfill clients, so it bodes well that they are the ones establishing the pace, instead of the group.

For example, a store comes up short on a famous item, for example, a child's grain brand. It risks losing clients. A few solutions exist to avoid this issue, such as: attempting to persuade clients to purchase another brand, which is risky and not practical; making huge supplies of the high-runner brand "in the event of some unforeseen issue", which is exorbitant from multiple points of view; or attempting to get the issue before it happens, which is the where

Kanban comes in. By showing a visual sign when the brand reaches a low stock level, the rack stocking employee knows to promptly discover a countermeasure with the Inventory Manager – no doubt submitting an emergency request with a supplier or purchasing simply enough things at retail cost to cover the day's interest. Notice that the client establishes the pace for requesting the product (cereal) which will in the long run lead to more production toward the start of the supply network. Later on, the Inventory Manager will take some time with his group to comprehend why they came up short on the item and experiment with new activities to guarantee that the issue doesn't happen once more. Kanban is hence the ideal device for connecting with individuals in settling concealed issues, and constantly attempting new, inventive activities to make increasingly, more value for clients.

As delineated in the model above, a Kanban is a sign sent by a downstream procedure that triggers a particular activity from an upstream procedure, for example, the recovery of parts, or the instruction to deliver a little unit of parts. The objective is to create just what is required, when it is required, and get as close as conceivable to the perfect of "sell one, make one". It regularly emerges as a card portraying what should be delivered or recovered, and including subtleties like source, goal, amount, here and there a date and time (on account of Kanban sent to providers).

In the digital and administration businesses, this framework works along these lines. A Kanban can appear as another item feature to create, a support request to deal with or a client request to satisfy. It speaks to the following "task" that must be finished currently so as to meet the day's objective. Since there is no decision but to finish this one request before going to the following one, individuals are urged to talk about issues and discover countermeasures to keep the Kanban descending down the "line". The point here isn't to punish individuals since they are not regarding the principles of Kanban, but to see the issue at the exact second it is going on, so we have a superior possibility of getting why and finding suitable countermeasures. Without these conversations on the Gemba and group critical thinking or problem solving activities, Kanban won't accomplish a lot. Individuals will rapidly return to pushing the flow the more reason that if they don't, nothing will be done and issues will stay covered up. Kanban is really a tool for creating and fortifying collaboration over the business by taking care of issues together (kaizen).

There are two significant perspectives to Kanban: production and material renewal. The goal of this creation part of Kanban is to adjust work process by flagging production of a section, segment, or subassembly just when the following activity in the process has started to take a shot at the unit or parcel recently delivered. Right now, material is gotten through the procedure in a synchronized manner. The item's compartment regularly fills in as the Kanban signal right now, a connected card giving extra data if necessary.

The material renewal part of Kanban, in which material is maneuvered into a work place from internal or external suppliers. These suppliers are required to give materials in the correct amount inside an assigned lead time. They have to do this dependably, reliably, and with the affirmation of high quality.

Kanban frameworks give a decent strategy to spotting what individuals are taking a shot at as opposed to dealing with the present request: did they detect a quality issue and would they say they are attempting to fix it as well as can be expected? Is it accurate to say that they are managing an issue on a past request that was sent back? It is safe to say that they are chipping away at something that was not arranged? Did a manager request that they take a shot at something different? Whatever the case might be, the issue will be rapidly unmistakable, so individuals can talk about and comprehend the explanations for it, and together discover an answer for refocus. There is constantly a valid justification why individuals get things done, as they regularly make up for loopholes all the while or gaps in information, and this is actually what is fascinating to comprehend. In a lean organization, takt-based work has priority over other work since it relates to the client request. Right now, Kanban is additionally the ideal solution for small scale management.

In any case, there are two conditions for this useful asset to work.

The first is that a Kanban must move within a constraint of time with the goal that everybody can see, initially, to what extent is left to satisfy this one client request or to manufacture this one item feature, and respond to hindrances before it's past the point of no return. For example, a development group that has five new product feature to construct, test and convey in seven days may set a 8-hour time limit on each component and make a visual line to deal with them each in turn, within the set time. Right now, a particular feature is a Kanban on the grounds that it shows the client request, much the same as requests in an eatery where the takt time ought to be the equivalent paying little mind to what number of individuals make up a table. Normally, for this to work, the advancement group must sort out what they would be delivering into clusters of comparative size, by either separating greater work units or pulling together them.

The second condition for Kanban to work is setting up an administration "chain of help". This implies administrators should ceaselessly bolster groups in settling dubious issues uncovered by the Kanban system. This is initially a sign of regard that adds to making mutual trust among administrators and employees. It is additionally an opportunity for business managers to find the pain points in the organization and the gaps in information so they can work with individuals on kaizen exercises and improve organization strategies. This requires a difference in mentality from chiefs who must help and challenge their groups as opposed to ordering and controlling them.

As organizations develop, they want to sort out exercises and individuals so they can give a predictable item or service to their clients. The inescapable downside is that useful storehouses structure, each with their own desire and style, and workers begin losing sight of who the genuine clients are. Kanban is an extraordinary instrument for making each individual in the organization closer to the final client and pulling together their consideration on making value. Think about a Kanban as a client thumping on your entryway and who needs to be served now, much the same as somebody strolling into an eatery and anticipating their nourishment on the table in no time. However, Kanban is only the beginning: it shows us the way to progress, so every individual can walk it on their own utilizing kaizen consistently. It is the key to making a genuine lean association.

The kaizen theory is a perspective. Also, there are numerous devices and techniques that help its execution throughout everyday life and in business. One such approach is Kanban. So when a business actualizes Kanban, it additionally utilizes the kaizen guideline of consistent improvement.

The Kaizen and Kanban approach assists businesses with finding their way to progress. Furthermore, after some time, distinguish bottlenecks that hinder their advancement and decrease profitability. At that point, find reasonable solutions and improve their procedure by making little, nonstop changes. Kaizen is the mystery fixing in the formula of being and remaining a Lean organization. Also, a similar way in which there is no lean without Kanban, there can be no Kanban without kaizen.

CHAPTER THREE

ADOPTING AND IMPLEMENTING KAIZEN AND KANBAN STRATEGY TO YOUR BUSINESS

KAIZEN ADOPTION

The quickened technological progressions, diminished item lifecycles, changing client needs, and the relentless worldwide competition that every day requests a more extensive assortment of items with the most elevated conceivable quality at quicker delivery times, are a portion of the difficulties that organizations face these days. These difficulties require proficient techniques to be confronted. As an absolute quality management and ceaseless improvement method, Kaizen outstands, on account of its straightforwardness and practicality.it is a tool that can be material to all levels, including our social and individual lives and, obviously, business. In the business setting, Kaizen advances a culture where all representatives — from the cleaning staff to the CEO—are urged to contribute. This consistent improvement technique was created in Japan after World War II. Receiving Kaizen implies accepting a consistent improvement culture that centers around waste and overflows disposal underway procedures. Kaizen suggests a steady test to improve standard. Truth be told, the articulation "a long journey starts with a little steps" plainly delineates the feeling of Kaizen. Each procedure of progress must be dynamic and start with a choice, and there is no turning around.

The quality control methods created by Edgard Deming is retaken by the Kaizen strategy and joins that our way of life and that of our businesses have the right to be continually improved. The message of the Kaizen methodology is that every day to day activities must be directed towards improvement, in the social setting, in our own lives, or while working. Additionally, being a conventionalist is the adversary of Kaizen. As in Just-in-Time (JIT), time in Kaizen is of vital significance, and in the business condition, it joins the management and procedure advancement, accentuating on client needs so as to recognize failures and boost time. The accomplishment of this ceaseless improvement concept in a business originates from its capacity to improve models in quality, costs, efficiency, or holding up times. This helps arrive at the best expectations.

Since 1980, Japanese firms, for example, Toyota, Hitachi, or Sony have become trustworthy instances of constant improvement of production forms. Correspondingly, Kaizen improvement and application are amalgamated with methods of operation management, mechanical designing, organizational behavior, quality, costs, upkeep, profitability, innovations, and logistics, among others. Researchers frequently discuss "the Kaizen umbrella," which is a lot of interrelated Lean manufacturing instruments and strategies, for example, total quality control, quality circles, suggestion system, automation, total productive maintenance (TPM), Kanban, quality improvement, Just-in-time (JIT), zero defects, little group activities, new product development (NPD), profitability improvement, order, and collaboration between Human Resource and managerial staff, among others.

IMPLEMENTING THE KAIZEN STRATEGY

The board must figure out how to execute certain fundamental ideas and frameworks so as to acknowledge kaizen system:

Kaizen and the management

Procedure versus result

Following the plan-do-check-act (PDCA)/standardize-do-check-act (SDCA) cycles

Putting quality first

Talk with information.

The following procedure is the client.

By method for presentation, top administration must advance a cautious and extremely clear statement of policy. It at that point they must set up an execution plan and exhibit leadership by rehearsing a kaizen methodology inside its own positions.

- Kaizen and Management

With regards to kaizen, the management have two significant capacities: maintenance and improvement. Maintenance alludes to exercises coordinated toward keeping up current innovative, administrative, and working standards and maintaining such gauges through training and order. Under its upkeep work, management plays out its relegated errands with the goal that everyone can adhere to standard working procedures (SOPs). Improvement, in the interim, alludes to exercises coordinated toward raising current standards or guidelines. The Japanese perspective on the management along these lines comes down to one statute: Maintain and improve standards or benchmarks.

Improvement can be named either kaizen or innovation. Kaizen means little enhancements because of progressing efforts. This innovation includes a radical improvement because of a huge investments of assets in new innovation or equipment. (At whatever point cash is a key factor, innovation is costly.) Because of their interest with development, Western managers will in general be fretful and ignore the long haul benefits kaizen can bring to an organization. Kaizen, then again, underscores human endeavors, spirit, communication, training, collaboration, involvement, and self-restraint—a practical, low-cost way to deal with progress.

- Procedure versus Result

  Kaizen encourages process-situated reasoning since processes must be improved for outcomes to improve. Inability to accomplish already planned outcomes shows a disappointment all the while. The executives must distinguish and address such errors which are process based. Kaizen centers around human endeavors—a direction that stands out from the outcomes based intuition in the West. A process-oriented methodology ought to be applied in the presentation of the different kaizen methodologies: the plan-do-check-act (PDCA) cycle; the standardize-do-check-act (SDCA) cycle; quality, cost, and delivery (QCD); total quality management (TQM); just-in-time (JIT); and total productive maintenance (TPM). Kaizen methodologies have bombed numerous organizations just in light of the fact that they overlooked process. The most pivotal component in the kaizen procedure is the responsibility and involvement of top administration. It must be shown quickly and reliably to guarantee achievement in the kaizen process.

- Following the PDCA/SDCA Cycles

  The initial phase in the kaizen procedure builds up the plan-do-check-act (PDCA) cycle as a vehicle that guarantees the congruity of kaizen in seeking after an approach of keeping up and improving norms. It is one of the most significant ideas of the procedure.

"Plan" alludes to building up an objective for development (since kaizen is a lifestyle, there consistently ought to be an objective for development in any region) and formulating plans or activity intending to accomplish that target. "Do" refers to executing the plan. "Check" alludes to deciding if the execution stays on target and has realized the improvement already planned. "Act" alludes to performing and institutionalizing the new systems to forestall repeat of the first issue or to set objectives for the new improvements. The PDCA cycle spins consistently; no sooner is an improvement made than the status-quo which results, turns into the objective for additional improvement. PDCA implies failing to be satisfied with status-quo, as usual. Since business employees lean toward the state of affairs and often don't have activity to improve conditions, the management must start PDCA by setting up persistently challenging goals or objectives. First and foremost, any new work process is unsteady. Before one begins chipping away at PDCA, any present process must be balanced out in a procedure regularly alluded to as the standardized-do-check-act (SDCA) cycle.

Each time a variation from the norm happens in the present procedure, the following inquiries must be posed: Did it happen because we didn't have a standard? Did it happen in light of the fact that the standard was not followed? Or on the other hand did it happen on the grounds that the standard was not sufficient? Simply after a standard has been built up and followed, settling the present procedure, should one proceed onward to the PDCA cycle. In this manner, the SDCA cycle institutionalizes and balances out the present procedures, while the PDCA cycle improves them. SDCA alludes to maintenance, and PDCA alludes to progress; these become the two significant obligations of the executives.

- Putting Quality First

Of the essential objectives of quality, cost, and delivery (QCD), quality consistently ought to have the most noteworthy need. Regardless of how appealing the cost and delivery terms offered to a client, the organization won't have the option to compete if the item or administration needs quality. Practicing a quality-first philosophy requires the management's responsibility since managers frequently face the impulse to make bargains in meeting delivery prerequisites or reducing expenses. In this manner, they risk yielding quality as well as the life of the business.

- Talk with Data

Kaizen is a problem solving and critical thinking process. All together for an issue to be accurately comprehended and tackled, the issue must be identified and the pertinent information assembled and broken down. Attempting to tackle an issue without hard facts or information is likened to depending on hunches and emotions—not a logical or objective approach. Gathering information on the present status causes you to comprehend where you are currently focusing; this fills in as a beginning stage for development. Gathering, confirming, and investigating information for development is a theme that is significant.

- The Next Process Is the Customer

All work is a progression of procedures, and each procedure has its supplier just as its client. A material or a snippet of data gave by process A (supplier) is dealt with and improved in process B and afterward sent on to process C. The following procedure consistently ought to be viewed as a client. The saying "the following procedure is the client" alludes to two sorts of clients: internal (inside the organization) and external (out in the market). The vast majority working in an organization make do with clients within the organization. This acknowledgment should prompt a responsibility never to pass on deficient parts or off base snippets of data to those in the following process. At the point when everyone in the organization keep to this adage, the outer client in the market, as a result, gets a great item or service. A genuine quality-affirmation framework implies that everyone in the organizations buys in to and rehearses this maxim.

KANBAN STRATEGIES/PROCESS

The most troublesome piece of changing any business procedure is normally the real execution of the new framework. In any case, the versatile and steady nature of Kanban ideas make frameworks utilizing these devices simpler to execute. Be that as it may, there are a few significant advances associated with appropriate execution of a Kanban framework.

Visualize the present work process

Catch current measurements and rules

Recognize bottlenecks

Set up another help level understanding (SLA) and approaches

Point of confinement work in progress (WIP)

Measure new lead times and some different measurements

- Visualize the Current Workflow

  The initial segment of the Kanban technique is to just imagine your real work process. Envision the work process implies that the group needs to portray and depict its procedure or value flow. This is achieved utilizing the Kanban and Kanban cards. The Kanban board, isolated in sections envisions the flow and every one of its stages. The Kanban cards shows the tasks. The cards development through the sections, shows the movement of value through the organization. The board has a double reason here. The undeniable one, following and checking the progress of the project. What's more, the second, recognizing bottlenecks and regions for development. Giving us the kaizen organization. Without an understanding of how the present procedure functions and how work is really played out, any conversation will be absolutely speculative. This is the reason the initial step will be to imagine the work process when you can.

This starts by recognizing the individual classes or paths of your delivery framework. Your genuine work items are separated into coherent pieces, every one of which is an item that is composed on a card. As work items course through the framework for delivery, these cards are in this way proceeded onward the Kanban board also.

- Set Work-in-Progress (WIP) Limits

A key part of Kanban approach is to confine the measure of Work in Progress (WIP) in any one path. Unequivocal points of confinement are set for every class, and work isn't permitted to be begun or maneuvered into a path if the measure of work in that path is as of now at its utmost. A procedure where work is started just when there are assets accessible to achieve the important undertakings is alluded to as pull booking. While it is essential to recognize regions of waste, it is considerably progressively critical to be wise in which procedures or activities to take a shot at simultaneously.

Constraining work-in-progress (WIP) is essential to executing Kanban – a 'Pull-framework'. By restricting WIP, you urge your group to finish work within reach first before taking up new work. Along these lines, work as of now in progress must be finished and checked done. This makes capacity in the framework, so new work can be pulled in by the group. At first, it may not be anything but difficult to choose what your WIP breaking points ought to be. Actually, you may begin with no WIP limits.

When you have adequate information, characterize WIP limits for each phase of the work process (every segment of your Kanban board) as being equivalent to a large portion of the normal WIP.

Ordinarily, numerous groups start with a WIP Limit of 1 to 1.5 times the quantity of individuals working in a particular stage. Restricting WIP and setting the WIP caps for every segment of the board not just helps the colleagues first complete what they are doing before taking up new stuff – yet additionally conveys to the client and different partners that there is constrained ability to accomplish work for any group – and they have to design cautiously what work they request that the group do.

The idea of the visual Kanban board normally makes any bottlenecks in the framework effectively noticeable. Back-log issues can be quickly seen and any means taken to address the issue would almost certainly be generally welcomed. Kanban promotes the spirit of collaboration towards tending to any Work in Progress back-log, and assets are regularly assigned so as to address any issues.

The time that each card remains in any lane, just as the time a card is standing by to move into a consequent lane ought to be recorded for examination. A key to successful Kanban use is to examine both the general procedure and the procedures inside every individual lane, with a definitive objective being to discover approaches to evacuate waste or inefficiencies that are recognized.

- Capture current measurements and rules.

    Without a decent comprehension of what the presentation of the present process is and whether the business clients are glad or not, any improvement endeavor will be perilous. Consequently, it will be critical to catch rules with respect to what has been going on. Instances of such rules could incorporate the following:

    a. All requests are conveyed somewhere in the range of six and twelve weeks.

    b. No advancement will be permitted before the main planner has given endorsement.

    c. All items ought to be tried by clients before being discharged into the market.

    d. A few clients are accessible just to perform client acknowledgment testing.

- Build up another SLA and policies.

  The purpose behind the possibility of SLA and approaches is to distinguish the business clients or clients' desires and what the two sides ought to do to find a workable level of execution with the goal that they can set up a relationship built on trust. For a case of SLA, we can envision that the group will ensure that every single new request will be delivered in about a month and a half. Consequently, the group could utilize this chance to necessitate that the clients be accessible three weeks before production to completely test all the new features. As far as new standards or arrangements, the group could conclude that they should chip away at administrative demands at first and deal with non-administrative things after.

- Analyze Work Flow and Make Improvements

  Estimation of objective is a significant piece of making upgrades to any business procedure or undertaking. This is likewise valid with any framework utilizing Kanban ideas. It is essential to recollect that Kanban isn't an upgrade of a current organizational framework. Kanban shows complements of the framework by making the assignments that an individual or group does, simpler by improving those tasks. There is no compelling reason to stress over having to start afresh and to totally change a procedure. In the event that specific pieces of tedious procedures are now working admirably, they won't be totally changed by executing a Kanban-based framework.

Utilize the important instruments of the Kanban boards to investigate the status of a procedure. A decent examination makes it conceivable to identify shortcomings, wastes and any changes that must be made. While a few frameworks that include organized project management, well structured, comes with risk in usage, Kanban comes with negligible risks due to its versatile nature. People and organizations searching for approaches to disentangle processes without facing the challenge of losing cash and time can profit by Kanban ideas.

Contingent upon how well the work process is characterized and WIP Limits are set, you will watch either a smooth flow inside WIP limits or work accumulating as something gets held up and begins to hold up capacity. The entirety of this influences how rapidly work crosses from start to the end of the work process (a few people call it value stream). Kanban enables your group to break down the framework and make changes in accordance to improve flow in order to diminish the time it takes to finish each bit of work.

A key part of this procedure of watching your work and settling/removing bottlenecks is to observe the intermediate hold up stages (the halfway Done stages) and perceive to what extent work items remain in these "handoff stages". As you will get the hang of, lessening the time spent in these hold up stages is critical to diminishing Cycle Time. As you improve flow, your group's conveyance of work becomes smoother and increasingly unsurprising. As it turns out to be increasingly unsurprising, it gets simpler for you to make dependable responsibilities to your client about when you will complete any work you are doing for them. Improving your capacity to estimate finish times dependably, is a major piece of actualizing a Kanban framework!

- Make Process Policies Explicit

As a component of visualizing your procedure, it is important to identify and visualize unequivocally, your approaches (process, rules or guidelines) for how you accomplish the task you do perform. By planning explicit process guidelines, you make a typical reason for all members to see how to do any sort of work in the system. The strategies can be at the board level, at a swim path level and for each column. They can be an agenda of steps to be accomplished for each work item-type, entry-exit criteria for every section, or anything at all that helps colleagues deal with the progression of work on the board well. Instances of explicit policies or strategies include the meaning of a completed task, the depiction of individual lanes or segments, who pulls when, and so on. The approaches must be explicitly defined and visualized for the most part on the top of the board and on every path and section.

- Implement Feedback Loops

Feedback loops are vital piece of any great framework. The Kanban Method energizes and encourages you to implement feedback loops of different sorts – survey stages in your Kanban board work process, metrics and reports and a scope of viewable signs that give you consistent input on work progress – or its absence – in your system. While the mantra of "Fail quick! Flop frequently!" may not be naturally comprehended by numerous groups, getting criticism early, particularly if you are on an inappropriate track with your work, is vital to having the correct work delivered, the correct item or service to the client in the most briefly conceivable time. Feedback loops are basic for guaranteeing that.

With Kanban, everything is centered around accomplishing ceaseless improvement. Learning assumes a definitive job. With the end goal for us to have the option to get the hang of something, we need criticism to identify what we can improve. For instance, numerous organizations settle on day by day stand-up meetings where input about the present work circumstance is passed across. There is suggestion that these meetings happen at the group level as well as for a bigger scope, including the whole value chain. The quantity of members can be limited by utilizing agents of individual groups to facilitate those of different groups before the board. Reviews, improvement meetings which are targeted, are additionally a significant mechanism of feedback. The following adage applies: the more extensive the spectrums of members, the better the feedback or criticism. Operational surveys are frequently utilized for organization-wide finding out about metrics. Whatever builds up high-quality feedback about the real procedure ought to be incorporated into the regular working practice so as to learn and improve.

- Improve Collaboratively, Evolve Experimentally (utilizing the scientific strategy)

The Kanban Method is a developmental improvement process. It encourages you embrace little changes and improve steadily at a pace and size that your group can deal with no problem at all. It energizes the utilization of the scientific technique – you structure a hypothesis, you test it and you make changes relying upon the result of your test. As a group actualizing Lean/Agile standards, your key task is to assess your procedure continually and continuously improve and as could be expected under the circumstances.

The effect of each change that you make can be watched and estimated utilizing the different signs your Kanban framework gives you. Utilizing these signs, you can assess whether a change is helping you improve or not, and conclude whether to keep it or have a go at something different. Kanban frameworks assist you with gathering a great deal of your framework's exhibition information – either physically, in the event that you utilize a physical board, or consequently, in the event that you utilize a particular tool, for example, SwiftKanban. Utilizing this information, and the measurements it helps you produce, you can without much of a stretch assess whether your presentation is improving or dropping – and change your framework as needed.

Improvement doesn't imply that we continually need to waste time. On account of numerous issues, we can make use of approaches and models that light up the sets of problems that continually return in all systems and have consequently effectively demonstrated their incentive. Kanban is itself an adjustment of accessible practices and beliefs—for instance, from the car business—for the reasons of programming development specifically and in general, knowledge work. There have been found some few fitting and well-proven hypotheses for the fundamental standards of Kanban, for example, previously mentioned theory of constraints; economic understandings of waste as exchange and coordination costs, for instance; or the impacts of changeability on a given system. All things considered, Kanban doesn't endorse which models and strategies must be applied. This is on the grounds that the requests and circumstances are diverse in each organization. Neither does Kanban endorse how models and techniques ought to be applied. No statements are made concerning what is correct and what's is probably wrong. Only for the different kinds of representation, there are now the same number of potential outcomes as there are businesses on the planet that apply Kanban.

- Design The Kanban System

Subsequent to dissecting and mapping out the procedures associated with the general task, the following stage is planning a Kanban board. For progressively complex business projects that incorporate a few sub-projects, make a few Kanban boards. Some portion of the structure procedure includes concluding who will finish various tasks. Choose what sorts of segments and columns to put on the Kanban board. It is ideal to set up cards to profit the general process. For instance, a card may have classes for different tasks, groups, workers and task of different priority levels. Consider how the Kanban board will look as individuals move task cards into segments for updates. Probably the greatest error individuals make when mapping a project and sorting out the procedures engaged with it, is envisioning a perfect task rather than the genuine process. Taking a look at the project equitably and practically makes it simpler to outline the undertaking in an ideal way. Start by mapping a procedure in its genuine existence. By taking a look at it and arranging all things considered, it is conceivable to keep away from pitfalls, identify waste and make any fundamental changes.

CHAPTER FOUR

BUSINESS PROCESSES AND

MANAGEMENT

VISUALIZATION

At the gemba (In business, the value adding exercises that makes the client satisfied, occur in the gemba), irregularities of assorted types emerge each day. Just two potential circumstances exist in the gemba: Either the procedure is leveled out, or it is out of control. The former implies smooth tasks; the latter means something bad. The act of visual management includes the clear display of gembutsu-the real item, also including charts, lists, and records of performance, so both administration and workers are persistently helped to remember all the components that make quality, cost, and delivery (QCD) fruitful—from a presentation of the general strategy, to production figures, to a rundown of the most recent worker suggestion. Therefore, visual management comprises a vital piece of the establishment of gemba.

- Making Problems Visible

  Issues ought to be made visible in the gemba. In the event that a variation from the norm can't be identified, it's not possible for anyone to deal with the procedure. In this way, the main standard of visual management is to highlight problems. In the event that rejects are being created by a die on a press and no one sees the rejects, there will before long, be a heap of rejects. A machine furnished with jidoka gadgets, nonetheless, will stop the minute a reject is produced. The machine stoppage makes the issue obvious. At the point when a reception guest goes to the front counter and requests an anti-inflammatory medicine or a rundown of good eateries close by, the lodging's failure to satisfy those requirements establishes an irregularity. By posting a rundown of the most continuous requests got from visitors, the management of the hotel can increase a consciousness of administration lacks that should be tended to. This is visual management: making variations from the norm noticeable to all employees—managers, directors, and workers—with the goal that remedial activity can start immediately. Most information starting from the gemba experiences numerous managerial layers before arriving at top administration, and the information turns out to be progressively abstract and remote from reality as it moves upward. Where visual management is drilled, in any case, an administrator can see problems initially, the minute the person in question strolls into the gemba and consequently can give directions on the spot, continuously. Techniques of visual management employees of gemba to take care of such issues.

The best thing that can occur in the gemba of a manufacturing organization is for the line to stop when an anomaly is identified. There's a statement that; a sequential construction system that never stops is either great (unimaginable, obviously) or incredibly awful. At the point when a line is halted, everybody perceives that an issue has emerged and tries to guarantee that the line won't stop for a similar reason, once more. Line stoppage is probably the best case of visual management in the gemba.

- Keeping in touch with Reality

In the event that the main purpose behind visual management's presence is to make issues visible, the second is to support both workers and managers remain in direct contact with the reality of the gemba. Visual management is a down to earth technique for deciding when everything is leveled out and for sending a notice the minute an irregularity emerges. At the point when visual management functions, everyone in the gemba can oversee and improve procedures to acknowledge QCD. At the point when clients go on voyages to business firms, the display boards are usually being shown that permit everyone to see the production timetable and how the work is advancing. The arrangements are distinctive for each firms or plant. Some make use of whiteboards, though others use paper; some use magnets, yet the display boards are in every case clear and straightforward, effectively serving the purpose of assisting the individuals by permitting them to keep in contact with reality on the gemba.

Visual Management in the Five Ms (5M)

The management must deal with the five Ms (5M) in the gemba: manpower, machines, materials, methods, and measurements. Any variation from the norm identified with the 5M conditions must be shown outwardly. What follows is a progressively itemized look at visual management in these five areas.

- Manpower (Operators)

  How is worker morale? This can be estimated by the quantity of recommendations made, the degree of interest in quality circles, and figures on non-attendance. How would you realize who is missing from the work or line today and who is having their spot? These things ought to be made visible at the gemba. How would you realize individuals' ability level? A presentation board in the gemba can show who is prepared to do what task and who needs extra training. How would you realize that the administrator is carrying out the responsibility right? Guidelines that demonstrate the correct method to carry out the responsibility—for instance, the one-point standard and the standard worksheet—must be shown.

- Machines

  How would you realize that the machine is delivering

acceptable quality items? If jidoka and pokayoke (mistake-proofing) devices are connected, the machine stops functioning immediately after something turns out badly. At the point when we see a machine that is halted, we need to know why. Is it halted on account of planned downtime? Changeover and set-up? Quality issues? Machine breakdown? Preventive fix? Oil levels, the recurrence of trade, and the kind of grease must be shown. Metal lodgings ought to be supplanted by covers which are transparent with the goal that operators can see when a glitch happens inside a machine.

Materials

How would you realize the materials are flowing easily? How would you know whether you have a larger number of materials than you can deal with and whether you are creating a larger number of number than you should? At the point when a minimum stock level is determined and Kanban—appending a card or tag to a cluster of work-in process as a method for communicating orders between forms—is utilized, such irregularities become visible. The location where materials are put away should be shown, together with the stock level and parts numbers. Various hues ought to be utilized to forestall botches. Utilize signal lights and sound signs to highlight abnormalities, for example, supply deficiencies.

- Methods

How does a manager know whether individuals are carrying out their responsibilities right? This is clarified by standard worksheets posted at every workstation. The worksheets should show succession of work, process duration, safety items, quality checkpoints, and what to do when there's occurrence of variability.

- Measurements

How would you check whether the procedure is running easily? Gauges must be plainly set apart to show safe working reaches. Temperature-detecting tapes must be joined to engines to show whether they are producing excess heat. How would you know whether an improvement has been made and whether you are enroute to arriving at the objective? How would you know if precision equipment is appropriately measured? Pattern diagrams ought to be shown in the gemba to show the quantity of suggestions, production plans, quality improvement targets, efficiency improvement, reduction of set-up time, and decrease in industrial accidents.

VISUAL MANAGEMENT WITH 5S

You likely have understood that visual management additionally has a great deal to do with the five stages of housekeeping. At the point when we take part in 5S, we find that its result is better visual management. Better housekeeping assists with making anomalies visible so they can be remedied.

The 5S techniques can be sorted out from the point of view of visual management:

- Seiri ("disposing of pointless things"). Everything in the gemba ought to be there if, and just if, it is required now or will be utilized in the prompt future. When you stroll through the gemba, do you find unused work-in-process, supplies, machines, instruments, dies, racks, trucks, compartments, archives, or personal effects that are not being used? Discard them with the goal that only what is required remains.

- Seiton ("putting in order that remain"). Everything in the gemba must be in the perfect spot, prepared for use when you need it. Everything ought to have a particular address and be set there. Are the lines on the floor marked appropriately? Are the lobbies liberated from snags? Once seiton is being practiced, it is anything but difficult to distinguish anything out of request.

- Seiso ("exhaustive cleaning of equipment and the area"). Are the equipment, floors, and dividers clean? Would you be able to recognize variations from the norm (e.g., vibrations, oil spillage, and so on.) in the equipment? Where seiso is drilled, any such variation from the norm ought to before long become obvious.

- Seiketsu ("keeping oneself perfect and dealing with the three going before things day by day"). Do representatives wear legitimate working garments? Do they use security glasses and gloves? Do they proceed with their work on seiri, seiton, and seiso as a piece of their every day schedule?

- Shitsuke ("self-control"). Every individual's 5S obligations must be indicated. Is it true that they are noticeable? Have you built up norms for them? Do workers adhere to such standards? The workers must record information on diagrams and check sheets on an hourly, every day, or week by week premise. As a method for cultivating self-control, the board may demand that laborers fill in information every prior day returning home. Great 5S in the gemba implies that as long as the machines are in activity, they are delivering acceptable quality items.

POSTING STANDARDS

At the point when we go to the gemba, visual management gives measures of performance. An abnormality is said to be seen when one finds exorbitant boxes of supplies on the line side, when a truck conveying supplies is left outside its planned zone, and when a passage is loaded up with boxes, ropes, rejects, and carpets. (A foyer is intended to serve just as an entry, not an area for storage.)

Showing work gauges before the workstation is visual management. These work norms not just help the worker to remember the correct method to carry out the responsibility but, progressively significant, empower the manager to decide if the work is being finished by standards. At the point when administrators leave their stations, we know there is an abnormality in light of the fact that the standard showed before the workstation indicate that the administrators should remain there during working hours. At the point when the operators don't complete their work inside process duration, we can't hope to accomplish the day's production target. While standards outline how workers ought to carry out their responsibilities, they frequently don't determine what move ought to be made in case of an abnormality. Guidelines should initially characterize anomalies and afterward plot the means to follow accordingly.

Production targets, daily, should be visible. Hourly and day by day targets ought to be shown on a board nearby the actual figures. This data makes the director aware of the measures important to accomplish the objective, for example, moving specialists to the line that is bogged down. All the dividers in the gemba can be transformed into instruments for visual management. The accompanying data ought to be shown on the dividers and at the workstations to tell everyone the present status of QCD:

Quality information—every day, week after week, and month to month dismiss figures and pattern graphs, just as focuses for development

Gembutsu ("real pieces") of rejects—for all administrators to see (These gembutsu are once in a while alluded to as sarashikubi—a word from medieval occasions meaning the "cut off leader of a criminal in plain view in the town square." These rejects are frequently utilized for preparing purposes.)

Cost data—efficiency figures, patterns, and targets

Worker hours

Conveyance data—every day creation graphs Machine vacation figures, patterns, and targets Overall equipment efficiency (OEE)

Number of recommendations submitted

Quality-circle exercises

For every specific procedure, any number of extra things might be required.

SETTING TARGETS

The third reason for visual management is to explain targets for development. Assume that external necessities have incited a plant to lessen the set-up time of a specific press inside a half year. In such a case, a display board is set alongside the machine. To start with, the present time set-up (e.g., six hours as of January) is plotted on a chart. Next, the objective value (one-half hour by June) is plotted. At that point a straight line is drawn between the points demonstrating the objective to focus on every month. Each time the press is set up, the time is estimated and plotted on the load up. Exceptional training must be given to assist workers with arriving at the objective. After some time, something mind boggling happens. The real set-up time on the diagram begins to follow the objective line! This happens on the grounds that the administrators become aware of the objective and understand that management anticipates that they should arrive at it. At whatever point the number hops over the objective, they realize that an anomaly (e.g., missing devices, and so forth.) has emerged and make a move to dodge such a setback later on. This is one of the most impressive impacts of visual management. Numbers alone are insufficient to propel individuals. Without targets, numbers are dead.

A definitive objective of progress is top administration's strategies. One of top management's jobs is to set up long and medium-term policies just as yearly strategies and to noticeably demonstrate them to employees. Regularly such strategies are displayed at the passageway to the plant and in the lounge area just as in the gemba. As these arrangements are separated into different levels of management that at long last, arrive at the shop floor, everyone will comprehend why it is important to take part in kaizen exercises.

Kaizen exercises become important in the brains of gemba individuals as they understand that their exercises identify with corporate systems, and a feeling of mission is imparted. Visual management assists with distinguishing issues and inconsistencies among targets and current real factors. As it were, it is a way to settle the procedure (upkeep work) just as improve the procedure (improvement work). Visual management is an amazing asset for rousing gemba individuals to accomplish administrative targets. It gives numerous chances to workers to fortify their own exhibition

through presentations of targets came to and progress made toward
objectives.

CHAPTER FIVE

BUSINESS IMPROVEMENT OPPORTUNITIES USING THE KAIZEN AND KANBAN STRATEGY

The most troublesome piece of an improvement procedure or problem solving and critical thinking exertion is regularly the initial step. In problem solving, the inability for a particular problem to defined in appropriate terms will regularly crash groups and prevent endeavors from pushing ahead. A comparable test exists in Kaizen. For development to happen, people engaged with the improvement procedure need to discover the underlying waste and begin to see the improvement potential. The initial step of Kaizen is an activity in helping people figure out how to see various sorts of waste, wastefulness, issues, and territories for development.

Before clarifying a portion of the normal tools and ideas used to encourage this initial step, let us first make a stride back and call attention to the contrast between problem solving and Kaizen. The two terms are frequently utilized conversely; notwithstanding, in Toyota they are concepts which are distinct. Ordinarily, the meaning of problem solving fixates on the principal thought of "gap" or "deviation from standard"). A standard may exist for cost, quality, profitability, conveyance, wellbeing, or any number of other such classifications. At the point when real estimations of the procedure go astray from the normal or arranged result, at that point a gap exists, and a problem is said to exist. Issues can generally exist in forms relying upon how the standard desire for performance is characterized. Some of the time, standard can be set excessively low, or after a timeframe the standard is routinely accomplished. What at that point happens when there is no hole from standard? Does this imply there is no requirement for development? This basic differentiation is a piece of the verifiable purpose behind the Toyota Kaizen abilities course. In any event, when a procedure is working at standard, we can at present, expect and drive improvement.

Measurements give us where the framework is "getting caught" how it has created, and where we have to change things so as to arrive at the stipulated objectives. Measurements bring us onto the correct track: they are the initial step. To be successful, we should obviously make real improvements. In any case, we should pose the accompanying inquiry before applying any exceptional techniques for development: Why is the circumstance the manner in which it is, in any case? Since, for instance, the hypothesis of limitations is too intense an approach or maybe even an inappropriate hypothesis if there are brief bottlenecks in our framework that just show up in the Christmas season. The reason for all improvement approaches is along these lines a profound comprehension of the issues.

The analysis of root cause presents causes and end results in direct connection to each other. One could be scholastic and plot cause-and-effect charts. In any case, there are far more straightforward and accordingly, much of the time increasingly powerful techniques for execution. If in a system, the equivalent undesired circumstances (side effects) are constantly seen, the easiest and most catalyst type of root cause investigation is to wonder why a couple of times. You start at the degree of the issue clear to everybody and work step-by-step in reverse until you arrive at the real reason. Just once we've distinguished the reasons for an issue and appropriately comprehended it, does it bode well to consider

the potential methods for fathoming it. As a rule, it is an issue of a meeting up of a few issues; in this way, the inquiry that continues emerging is whether a potential arrangement comprehends the "right" issue—does it truly create an enduring change, or does it just require the manifestations incidentally to be postponed?

Bottlenecks, Waste Elimination, and Reduction of Variability

Every one of these models for improvement has been completely investigated and created in its own assemblage of information. Everyone has its own way of thinking on persistent improvement. With Kanban, these three models are blended to give an outline of how to perceive these improvement openings, and subtletico on the best way to execute upgrades utilizing each model. Every one of the three ways of thinking on constant improvement depicted, has its own gathering of thought leaders, its own meetings, its own standard of information and experience, and its own gathering of supporters. Your organization may buy in to at least one of these schools. Having the option to show how Kanban's procedures can give chances to progress in your organization's preferred flavor might be a favorable position. Realizing that you have a wide arrangement of progress standards and tools to look over ought to give more prominent adaptability to make change.

Theory of constraints

This theory depends on the systems theory perception that the throughput of a framework is only dictated by one restricting variable. We can possibly improve the throughput if the entire framework beginning with this restricting variable is thoroughly optimized. To this end, Goldratt's five focus steps is duly referenced, which is the core of our treatment of bottlenecks. Just one of these five stages is ever utilized in numerous organizations—the attempt to augment the bottleneck by heaping more assets into it. In Goldratt's plan, in any case, this is the fourth of the five stages and should just be done once the initial three stages are finished. In reality, business projects don't get speedier if more assets are contributed on a short-term premise. The extra assets should right off the bat be found (e.g., new workers). At that point the new assets need a measure of time to get built up, for instance, training new colleagues. Such activities are bound to expand the lead time further as opposed to diminish it. What potential improvement can the theory of constraints get in the setting of Kanban if the five stages are appropriately followed?

Recognizable proof of the bottleneck. Kanban makes this progression exceptionally simple for us since we can rapidly recognize where things are clogging up the framework utilizing our visualization. We should anyway recall the underlying root cause analysis again. Do we have a genuine lasting bottleneck on the board before us? Just once this inquiry has been addressed should a bottleneck really be treated as such.

There are then two further classes of waste we can handle:

- Transaction costs: These incorporate the preliminary and follow-up ventures that collect around a task, that is, arrangement exercises, planning of projects, asset arranging, risk planning, delivery, client preparing, reviews, surveys, and so forth.

- Coordination costs: These incorporate the occasionally enormous costs that ineffectively arranged and severely directed gatherings of numerous types cause. Probably the least expensive improvement that can be actualized is to complete gatherings effectively. Every day stand-up gatherings can be decreased to 10 min, for instance, and specialized inquiries can be moved to follow up gatherings so as to not tie up the assets of the uninvolved workers superfluously. This saves time limits in which work should be possible on the client's task.

During the 1990s, the Theory of Constraints advanced a strategy for the analysis of root cause and change the board known as the Thinking Processes (or TP). The purpose behind this advancement was the revelation among the TOC consulting community that their imperative on accomplishing improvement with customers was having the management changed and resistant to change. It appeared that the Five Focusing Steps just seemed to function admirably for flow problems and that numerous work environment challenges didn't fit perfectly into the paradigm of flow. So TP advanced. The expert capability and preparing program for TOC specialists transformed from a class on the utilization of the Five Focusing Steps and its applications, for example, Drum-Buffer-Rope, to a class on TP. Subsequently, numerous in the TOC people group, when alluding to TOC, are in certainty alluding to TP and not the Five Focusing Steps. On observation of TOC gatherings, utilization of the Five Focusing Steps among the TOC people group has become to some degree an under-appreciated skill. The TOC community group has, from what has been seen, would in general acknowledge accept paradigms as they are built up instead of challenge them. Henceforth, the TOC solution for management of project, Critical Chain, advanced around the occupant project management worldview of the triple constraint (scope, spending plan, and schedule) and the reliance chart model for planning the assignments in a task. Nobody tested the incumbent model.

The expression "waste" is gotten from lean creation and presumably has a fairly negative undertone for some readers. To diminish waste doesn't intend to savagely dispose of everything that doesn't carry extra an incentive to the clients. It implies the optimization of exercises that we ourselves must set up for the execution of a task, so that the least expenses are created (as far as both time and cash). So we question the value formation of our exercises, "does it produce extra value for the client if we accomplish a greater amount of this?" Three additional gatherings are of no utilization to the client or the association itself if nothing substantial outcomes from them.

Reducing variability

By variability, we mean deviations from the standard work process. The greater variability a framework displays, the harder it is to give dependable information about lead times. As opposed to the get together industry with its planned machines, information work, because of the human will, will consistently have an elevated level of variability. The inquiry is whether this inconstancy ought to be decrease to the basic or whether fluctuation maybe likewise contains its own latent capacity. This is reserve limit with respect to crises, improvers, and trend-setters who can productively resolve the feeble focuses in a framework and transform them into qualities, while the others worry about the standard day by day work. At last, diminishing haziness is gainful just in zones where this fogginess itself causes issues, for instance, in situations where we need to settle on service-level concurrences with our clients and have an exceptionally elevated level of changeability in the culmination of the occupations. What's a client expected to do when confronted with, "The fulfillment time for the activity is somewhere close to one and 100 days."? The activity could be prepared • Absence of WiP limits for task types • Limits on the different classes of administration that are excessively high (e.g., too many express tickets) • Too much time fixing mistakes because of bugs • A clogged-up work process due to too many blocked tickets with all the examinations and different instruments that

Kanban makes accessible, we can discover what causes changeability in our framework and what sway it has. Be that as it may, changeability shouldn't be diminished only for lessening it. On the off chance that it is troublesome and bargains associations with clients, it ought to be confined to a level that is mediocre. In any case, we should likewise become accustomed to the possibility that fluctuation is a basic attribute of information work. We need to improve execution in the realm of work with Kanban. We're not keen on raising programming Jedis ready to program perpetually in diminishing measures of time with the goal that more occupations can be taken on or shortcoming disregarded. Kanban doesn't consider an individual a powerless point yet, watches the framework wherein we work as a system of cooperation that occasionally encounters issues. Utilizing its instruments, Kanban transforms its clients into framework masterminds who perceive and see how various methodologies impact one another. Members start to think as far as procedures instead of secluded people and don't see only high contrast yet rather all the shades in the middle. With time, it will become more clear that everything in a framework is associated and has a claim job in the general function.

FOCUSING STEPS

Focusing Steps' make emphasis on bottlenecks. The union of TOC with Lean enabled upgrades in venture and performance of organization and established the framework for the development of Kanban. Any procedure or work process that includes division of work can be characterized as a value stream; and any value stream can be seen to have flow. Lean and the Toyota Production System are basically worked around this supposition. If any value stream has flow, at that point the Five Focusing Steps can be applied to it. Henceforth, the Five Focusing Steps is a splendidly palatable POOGI, and TP isn't required except if you are utilizing it as a change management instrument.

Five Focusing Steps

The Five Focusing Steps is a basic recipe for a procedure of continuous improvement. It states:

- Distinguish the constraint.

- Conclude how to abuse the imperative.

- Subordinate everything else in the framework to the choice made in Step 2.

- Elevate the constraint.

- Maintain a strategic distance from inactivity; recognize the following limitation and come back to stage 2.

Stage 1 is requesting that we discover a bottleneck in our value stream. Stage 2 requests that we recognize the potential throughput of that bottleneck and contrast that with what is really occurring. As you will see, the bottleneck is seldom or never working at its full limit. So ask, "What might it take to get the maximum capacity out of our bottleneck? What might we have to change to get that going?" This is the "choose" portion of stage 2.

Stage 3 requests that we roll out whatever improvements are important to execute the ideas from stage 2. This may include rolling out extra improvements somewhere else in the value stream so as to get the most extreme limit from the bottleneck. This activity of amplifying the bottleneck's ability is known as "exploiting the bottleneck." Step 4 recommends that if the bottleneck is working at its full capacity is still not delivering enough throughput, its capacity should be improved so as to expand throughput. Stage 4 also requests that we actualize an improvement to upgrade ability and have throughput increase, adequately with the goal that the present bottleneck is soothed and the framework limitation moves somewhere else in the value stream. Stage 5 necessitates that we give the progressions time to balance out and afterward recognize the new bottleneck in the worth stream and repeat the procedure. The outcome is an arrangement of consistent improvement wherein throughput is continually expanding. In the event that the Five

Focusing Steps is standardized appropriately, a culture of constant improvement will have been accomplished all through the organization.

Fitting Kanban to Your Company Culture

In the event that your organization is a Six Sigma organization, Kanban can assist you with running Six Sigma activities in the product, frameworks, item improvement, or Information Technology organization. If your organization is a Lean organization, Kanban is a characteristic fit. Also, your organization buys in to and utilizes the Theory of Constraints, Kanban can empower a whole constraints-management (bottleneck-expulsion) program in your product, frameworks, item advancement, or IT association. In any case, you may need to rework the implementation of the pull system as a Drum-Buffer-Rope execution as opposed to allude to it as Kanban framework. Since Kanban created from a prior Drum-Buffer-Rope usage, this will work.

CHAPTER SIX

IMPROVING BUSINESS SALES OR PRODUCTS

Attempt to think about the most exceedingly terrible and conceivable item you've at any point seen—possibly not as far as quality, yet simply some item no one in his correct brain might want to claim. The truth of the matter is: you don't have the foggiest idea whether the groups making those items are the most Agile groups ever. They may be doing the entire arrangement of Agile practices, have astounding mentors, and improve their procedure persistently. In any case, they are being advised to make an item no one needs, and they are complimented when they convey it. Some may contend 'this isn't Agile' on the grounds that there is no evident client agent, only one individual who thinks he recognizes what the market needs, and, if the visionary falls flat, that is not an issue for Agile item advancement: we were simply building up an inappropriate item in an Agile manner. Some others may likewise contend that you couldn't have cared less to comprehend an incentive from the client point of view—obviously, your client, the one paying for the improvement, may be this visionary. My answer, regardless, is what difference does it make? In the event that Agile or Lean are not to be accused for idiotic items, fine, no issue from my side. In any case, we despite everything have the issue of building up an inappropriate item in an Agile or Lean manner, so perhaps we need to look elsewhere to remember an item point of view for the Kaizen culture—I mean, on the off chance that you care about the endurance of your organization, obviously.

Think about another improvement zone: client assistance. Lithe doesn't reveal to you how to improve that. Much more terrible: client assistance is viewed as waste under a Lean point of view—it ought to be diminished to the base through great quality items and great item documentation or preparing. Truth be told, client care necessities going to an Agile group are normally viewed as setting exchanging and a danger to group center. In any case, even Toyota must run client care lines, and client assistance is one of the most important elements customers survey while picking between various providers—so there's in reality some incentive in giving great client assistance.

The item point of view isn't just about the item itself: it likewise incorporates approaches to arrive at your customers and how to deal with your offer. You may have the best item on earth, yet on the off chance that your customers don't think about it your organization will likely fizzle. In the event that you are giving some web administration yet individuals don't have a clue about that your site exists, that doesn't imply that you neglected to get worth or how to improve your item—you neglected to improve your showcasing. As we will find right now, pipe improvement ought to be likewise a subject of Kaizen.

The fact I'm attempting to make here is that procedure improvement and group improvement are not the entire story: you need to think about your item, your client support, and your promoting system as well. Furthermore, with regards to item or administration improvement, it isn't about proficiency, time, and measurements.

Starting with a Vision

This starts with the client's point of view. Products or items which are successful can tackle a client's problem and furnish him/her with some value that different other options or workarounds—including just not taking care of the issue and becoming accustomed to it—don't give. Some business enterprise books and specialists instruct you to discover an issue that your client has and attempt to understand and also, trying to solve it. Obviously, to do such, you have to figure out who your customers are. What's more, in the event that you don't have the foggiest idea what your item is, how might you figure out who your customers are? You likely shut an endless loop.

Everything begins with a vision. The vision must be a convincing proclamation that pronounces what an organization will be about. It doesn't depict the item or business model, yet it makes way for every exertion in item management—including client development, item advancement, and item improvement.

The issue is that most 'statements of purpose's or 'key vision' archives are brimming with popular expressions, advisor talk, and corporate babble. The vision ought to be a little explanation, and be clear and essential. A five-to-ten word, action word target-result group is a decent method to begin. Think about Google's essential vision, 'sort out the world's data and make it all around open and helpful'. Here, the activity is to compose, the objective is the world's information, and the result is that it will be all around accessible and useful. A similar configuration has been effectively utilized by numerous world-class organizations. A few examples include: 'discover and find anything you should purchase on the web' (Amazon) or the one by John F. Kennedy: 'Put a man on the moon and bring him back alive before the decade's end' (NASA).

Another issue with numerous visions is that they are not about the client by any means. Consider Ford's statement of mission: 'An energizing viable Ford conveying productive development for all'— how is this important to their customers? Or then again for another model, ExxonMobil's statement of mission: 'ExxonMobil Corporation is focused on being the world's head oil and petrochemical organization. Keeping that in mind, we should constantly accomplish unrivaled monetary and working outcomes while holding fast to the best expectations of business direct'. As you see, it's not about their clients, yet about them getting more noteworthy, greater, and progressively gainful. On the off chance that you drive those sorts of vision into your corporate culture, your kin are not liable to think about an incentive from a client's point of view—except if they think about their partners as their fundamental clients, which is by all accounts the case. There can be a few dreams of the organization—side-effect, by brand, by regions—and they can change after some time. Be that as it may, such a large number of vision messages may get befuddling and even make logical inconsistencies, accordingly harming colossally your corporate culture and your item the executives' endeavors.

Product Space Versus Problem Space

One key attribute of good vision proclamations, other than including some client esteem explanation, is to give data on the issue we are attempting to tackle while not focusing on some random arrangement. This is the thing that I call 'issue space' considering rather 'arrangement space' thinking. At the point when John F. Kennedy asked NASA to put a man on the moon and bring him back alive before the decade's end, he was not endorsing any methods for doing as such. He simply depicted the issue to be understood and left the solution related choices to the item supervisory crew. There is an extremely mainstream urban legend about the Americans planning a million-dollar ball-point pen that could write in zero-gravity. In the interim, the Russians utilized a pencil in space. While the genuine story isn't actually similar to that, the purpose of the urban legend is to show how you can be frightfully off-base if you slip from issue space (write in zero gravity) to space for solution (pen that can write in zero gravity) and simply just care about the item, the item, the item.

Having thoughts just concerning the item can cause awful errors. In Spanish there's an adage: 'if you were born into the world a mallet, all you see is nails'. In any event, when gone up against with a client who has fasteners, you will attempt to utilize a sledge rather than a screwdriver since you are thinking in product space, not problem space.

Most systems and standards of production are dependent on simply 'preparing prerequisites' can prompt colossal waste and unneeded items. If there is no client appraisal and backing during the issue examination and solution structure, the client may very well accept that whatever he is requesting, will take care of his concern, and he may not be right. Then again, if there is no approval of the client problem solution suppositions before we race into advancement mode, we may be building proficiently and rapidly, something no one needs.

The well-known axiom, 'clients are the ones running our organization', implies that the organization should concentrate on client values; however, your clients are not really answerable for your item management process. In the best cases, as we will see straightaway, clients will be a piece of the team for product management. In those cases, simply doing 'whatever the customer says' ought to be considered as a dysfunction of the team.

The center suppositions—those that, whenever refuted, would nullify your entire plan of action—are those identified with the client- problem-solution articulation:

– Who is your client? Is there any market division? Are there various types of clients? Is there any important information about the clients that can impact the manner in which we take care of their issues?

– What is the issue we are attempting to settle? How would we realize it is an issue? How are clients right now managing that issue? Are there any workarounds? Are there some other items or arrangements our clients are utilizing to manage that issue? What are their key advantages and their primary defects?

– What solution can be provided that is superior to whatever other arrangement that the client is utilizing at the present time? What is the incentive and the key bit of leeway? By what means will we realize we are correct?

Anybody in the organization ought to have the option to answer the 'for what reason are we building this' inquiry concerning services and products—and the appropriate response 'due to the fact that the customer/the supervisor says as much' just prompts unremarkable and undesirable items, notwithstanding terrible corporate societies and low worker commitment. Recollect that one of the most acknowledged meanings of value in Agile/Lean environment is 'conformance to customer desires', so as to incorporate quality with the product, you should superbly comprehend those clients expectations.

Much more—you ought to deal with those desires and go about as a value advisor for your customer, too often your customer will be in item space thinking—'I came to you since I need this item'— rather than product space thinking—'I came to you since I have this issue'. In the event that your customer is requesting for a product that is wrong and such client expectations

are met, you may characterize that as 'quality' or should guarantee that it's not your issue—I couldn't care less: I see next to no esteem and an excessive amount of waste.

The Client Is Also Part of Your Team

Presumably, one of the most important and incredible, yet disregarded standards remembered for the Agile manifesto is 'client cooperation over contract negotiations'. Making the customer join your advancement group is definitely not another practice that is new. There is only sometimes, obvious instances of productive coordinated effort between improvement groups and their clients. More often than not, there is a customer intermediary or client agent as an item owner, product manager, or—surprisingly more dreadful—project supervisor. Not on the grounds that project management is awful or wrong be that as it may, to be completely forthright, managers of project will in general be progressively worried about assignments, deadlines, and cost than consumer loyalty, showcase achievement, or seeing genuine customer needs. You could contend this is 'awful' venture the board and you would be correct—we should leave it here with that basic comprehension.

There's next to no client joint effort in most Agile groups. What's surprisingly more dreadful: the customer is frequently observed as the foe. He intrudes in the group, requests changes, but then he's never accessible for explanation, approval, or obstacle evacuation. As a rule, the individual from the client's organization who collaborates with the development group is not the client, yet somebody dealing with the project from the client's side. This presents a great deal of commotion and invalid suspicions—or presumptions that are approved by an inappropriate individual, which is simply equivalent to approving them. This circumstance is what is termed ; 'creating items for an individual', as in the individual doesn't generally have a clue what the issue is about, nor he can furnish us with genuine bits of knowledge on the client problem-solution presumption—he's simply been appointed to convey a component list on a budget plan and deadline and he needs to accomplish this with the least conceivable agony and exertion.

Probably the most significant hindrances to group client collaborative effort are:

– Lack of trust/straightforwardness: the organization fears that, if the client is continually working together with the group, he will discover terrible quality issues, shrouded defects or some other sort of awful practices. A kind of 'black box Agile' is made where the client can't perceive what's going on inside the development process.

– 'Us versus them' syndrome: this generally happens when the organization or the group have been given bad names by customers in the past and, rather than creating practices and aptitudes to valuably manage these circumstances, they simply like to kick the customer out of their business environment and limit their collaborations—which obviously brings immense risks into advancement itself, however make their lives increasingly comfortable for the time being. Another form of this issue is the 'domineering client', which again implies the failure of the organization or the group to manage such circumstances.

– No Agile arrangement: the client isn't worried about Agility or might have been utilizing a waterfall-ish approach sufficiently long to consider that the correct method for dealing with a development project is to create an exceptionally detailed up-front requirement document —the 'Large Design Up-Front', BDUF. From that point forward, he accepts that his piece of the business project is done until the last achievements arrive and he shows up again to check everything against the requirements document. This conduct may likewise be recognized as an absence of client contribution.

– Bureaucracy and enormous clients: this is an uncommon instance of no Agile alignment. The client may really need to team up, but the organization requests that a lot of desk work, gatherings, reports and approvals occur in any event, for the slightest decision. This may be characterized as an absence of empowerment problem.

– No real client/absence of client involvement: the client's project administrator or representative isn't generally concerned or engaged with the project success. The explanations behind that include the customer needing to push all duty to the supplier, or the customer's delegate not being truly influenced by the task or item, so the individual in question considers it to be a weight in excess more than a challenge, a chance, or a piece of their obligation.

– Lack of focus: the client's agent is truly ready to help and work together with the improvement procedure, yet is simply excessively occupied. The reason is that coordinated effort with the development group is certifiably not a genuine priority, which likewise implies that the client doesn't see genuine value or the competitive advantage of client-team cooperation.

– Lack of client abilities: the client needs to work together, yet he does not have the necessary skills or aptitudes for collaboration. It may imply that there isn't sufficient support, training and assistance for the development group—including the customer.

– Geographical dispersion: This is an issue in the center land between lack of focus and absence of abilities. The customer can't move to the supplier's office, or the other way around, and there isn't sufficient involvement with utilizing remote joint effort tools and practices.

– Too numerous representatives: various people from the client's organization are giving distinctive information and at times negating one another—this is typically a process issue; a compelling cooperation system ought to be authorized before the task begins.

There are no simple answers for these issues. Understanding what precisely is your case—if it is depicted by at least one of the above reasons, and which of them—may assist you with identifying a suitable improvement plan.

Some generally useful activities that you should execute so as to upgrade client coordinated effort are:

– Ensure Agility first: If there is an attempt to make our customer join the development group too immediately, even before we can execute the most simple pieces of any Agile structure with least of effectiveness, the outcomes may be terrible and keep such customer from attempting once more.

– If conceivable, make it gradual: you may begin with meetings held bi-weekly to audit the outcomes and the arrangement. Afterward, you can begin requesting that your client go to some Kaizen events or every day meetings. As the customer begins to understand the value of those, he may be simpler to convince so as to acquire more joint effort from his side.

– Establish a typical joint effort structure: an exceptionally normal issue is that organizations make an incentive or attempt to seal the deal that is fixated on innovation, features, cost, and deadlines, however, they neglect to include some information for how the project is to be performed, directed, and managed. In the event that we truly comprehend Agile as a key piece of our organization, we ought to be prepared to clarify in our value proposition how working more on Agile way will help both the customer's organization and our own to augment the return on investment in a success win-win relationship. Then again, contracts, project charters, and project kick-offs should cultivate conversation on what is normal from the customer's side as far as dedication and obligation. The coordinated effort structure should not only describe an Agile improvement process, yet in addition, include descriptions of shared duties, the client agent's job, how to oversee changes, or how to manage conflicts and arrive at an accord.

– Make sure everybody comprehends this system toward the start of the project: continually convey the task's guidelines or joint effort structure and, if necessary, ensure there is adequate training and support accessible for your customer—it ought to be a piece of your value proposition

– Demand good representation: one of the key purposes of the collaboration system ought to be to have one representative who is empowered and from the client's side with both capacity to give access to any resources that may be required in the improvement process and to tackle any question between other client delegates, guaranteeing that, if necessary, there will be a solitary contact point for prioritization and explanation.

– Don't disregard soft skills: managing conflicts with your clients may be precarious, considering that their apparent force is path more noteworthy than the team's. Train everybody in peaceful correspondence, managing strife and productive contention before sending them to discuss with the customer.

– Follow Up: As with everything Kaizen, day by day follow-up of client collaboration significantly improves your odds of progress.

Consider the possibility that the client dismisses the collaboration terms. From several experiences and in multiple times, the client will really neglect to work together. This will happen either transparently—he will reject to go to meetings or give input—or in a progressively unobtrusive way—he will guarantee anything, however will neglect to satisfy hopes.

Notwithstanding the proof, it is still difficult to be liberal with the circumstances where customers neglect to work together with the improvement groups. It is believed that the principal reason is that we neglect to clarify and show on both the practical and rational levels, all the benefits the customer gets if such client is associated with the improvement process. Be that as it may, obviously, as a person, the customer is likewise dependent upon the hard-wiring of the mind, and will incline toward the quick reward of not being required to chip away at the project to the deferred delight of better outcomes.

In the event that the root cause for absence of client contribution is the client's outlook, the evangelizing and training efforts performed by the Kaizen specialists will take another dimension: it's never again enough to persuade the organization, there's need to push the message past its limits up to the client—and suppliers.

One vital perspective that ought to be upheld by the client collaboration system is to have the option to share both task benefits and misfortunes. There are a few 'Agile contract' approaches. An important one is that which includes mechanism to share risks and results. 'Fixed time, scope, and costs' agreements push all hazard to the supplier, yet on the opposite side 'time and materials' agreements will push all the risk to the client. None of these structures cultivate trust and joint effort. A mutual hazard approach will isolate benefits if the undertaking runs easily, or misfortunes if there are any postponements or unforeseen issues in it, consequently giving your client a motivating force to be engaged with the improvement and great administration of the project.

Knowing Your Client Is Knowing Your Product

How would we set up this? If there is a convincing vision as portrayed above, taking a shot at your client-problem-solution proclamation is a decent place to proceed. A few organizations contend that they as of now have set up products with long-term clients, so they don't see the point in restating the customer-problem-solution recommendation. Likewise, they don't think of them as assumption in the sense of hypothesis that should be tried.

Markets change. Innovation changes. Clients change. Issues change. Consider your client-problem-solution to be something static or given, and set yourself up for the ride—downwards.

So as to improve how your groups comprehend your client-problem-solution proclamations, there are a few exercises and tools you can utilize:

– Impact Mapping is a tool that is getting very well-known inside the Agile framework. Structured as a vital technique for planning. Impact Mapping begins with the 'why' of whatever the task, item, service, or activity one is examining—as it were, it begins with vision and purpose When we can portray the reason and make presumptions about our incentive, it encourages us figure out who can assist us with accomplishing our objectives (or prevent us from doing as such), what would they be able to do to help/stop us, how they can really help/stop us, and what can be done.

Jeff Patton's Story Mapping is likewise an extraordinary method to get familiar with your clients, given that they take an interest in the Story Mapping meeting. Through Story Maps, improvement groups can become familiar with the proposed excursion of their clients while utilizing the item and can participate in discussions about value, needs, and client needs.

– User journeys and user personas are notable systems for the user experience (UX) community. Popularized by UX master Alan Cooper, client personas are fictional characters used to comprehend the archetypes, market segments, demographics and particularities of various clients—rather than 'the client' articulation that accept that all users or purchasers of the products will carry on a similar way. Having your group construct client personas and, later on, talking with genuine clients that should coordinate our persona presumptions is an extraordinary method for creating insights into how to more readily unravel our clients' needs.

– Empathy Maps are additionally mainstream in the Agile and Lean Startup community Portrayed by Dave Gray and others in Game storming and later incorporated in Alex Osterwalder's Business Model Generation, this method searches for a more profound comprehension of partners in the business environment by investigating what they think, feel, say, and do.

– The Inception Deck is being utilized by an ever increasing number of groups as an extraordinary method for project or product chartering before going into 'full improvement mode'. Presented by Jonathan Rasmusson in The Agile Samurai, this assembles a lot of tools and techniques planned for making better attention to the objectives of the product, the reason, who the clients are, what the item is and isn't about, etc.

As you see, these systems, tools, and strategies are fundamentally attempting to answer the client-problem-solution statement in such a way that upgrades mindfulness and comprehension, by owner of the product /administrator/master, but from everybody in the organization. Regardless of what one prefers with regards to systems or techniques, simply ensure these reflections are made, and that they are followed up and previewd intermittently.

CHAPTER SEVEN

OPERATING AND

COORDINATING YOUR

BUSINESS

Up until this point, you've read a great deal about the instruments that help a Kaizen and Kanban group visualize and control its work process and shorten its lead times. Presently, obviously, you're likely asking how the group coordinates with its individuals and others. How work arrive at the group in a Kanban framework? Who chooses which work items land in the input queue? Who chooses what goes into the next release? Also, how? Kanban is a pure form of communication. We envision the work and pull work over a board—even this itself is a kind of communication. In any case, regardless of whether, or in reality since, we make heaps of things obvious, this methodology in a general sense obliges us to do one thing just: converse with one another. Individuals distinguish blockers, bottlenecks, or different issues utilizing the visualization. They start to examine things and search for solutions together. Kanban is accordingly sustained to an exceptionally huge degree by communication between colleagues. As a matter of fact, there's just concentration on one area of the whole value chain, yet every Kanban group ought to be impeccably clear about the way that

Kanban isn't a tool for self-gain; rather, it is the whole business that should benefit from Kanban. Together with the discussions that are at any rate created inside the group, this functions most importantly through communication with the up- and downstream stages at the limits of the group's segment of the value chain. The organized type of communication for the operation and coordination of a Kanban framework is consequently meetings.

Similarly, that Kanban recommends little except a couple of standards, it additionally doesn't direct that meetings must occur, what sort of gatherings they ought to be, or in what way these meetings should happen. In ordinary practice, the main thing that has end up being of significance is that during the transformative strides of progress there is consistently the requirement for periodical conversations and increasingly escalated communication with different partners of the present activity. The littlest change that would be encouraged is for the organization is to implement in this area, day by day stand-up meeting. For some boundless explanation, in information work, there are not many or no daily morning conversations for the coordination of the day's worth of effort. This isn't the situation underway (or, e.g., in emergency clinics), where it is and consistently has been standard to start the workday or the move by having the employees educate each other of work items to be finished. In doing as such, these organizations stay away from unnecessary copy and pointless work that is both inefficient and costly.

Together with the day by day stand-up meeting, we recommend a couple of different gatherings that have end up being helpful for Kanban activities, despite the fact that they are in no way, mandatory:

• Queue renewal meetings

• Release planning meetings

• Team retrospectives

• Operations reviews

We need to build up a particular delivery system in Kanban activities. We additionally need to keep away from waste—and time is what is frequently squandered. So as to limit coordination costs, meetings should occur at customary interims, consistently in a similar spot and simultaneously.

DAILY STAND-UP MEETINGS

In the day by day stand-up meeting, the group examines and sorts out the work items for the day, breaks down blockers, and searches for approaches to evacuate them. Visualization utilizing the board as a rule shows the work process situation correctly. The group meets at the load up each day at a fixed time and works through the items for work, methodicallly. In spite of the fact that we read from left to right, groups frequently intuitively start the conversation with the work in the far-right segment on the board, that is, with those that are about to be completed—the impact of the inclination that it is smarter to have originally finished one work item before starting the following is here obvious. Specific consideration is given to work that hasn't advanced in quite a while or has been obviously set apart as "blocked." It frequently occurs, for the most part with mature teams, that the blocked tickets are examined only. The groups talk about what the causes are and which worker at what particular point of the work process can help. Also, anybody requiring help can present their solicitation. With regards to the daily stand-up gatherings, the group can explain whether all tickets are advancing inside the concurred service-level understandings or whether the class of administration of individual tickets should be changed.

During the everyday stand-up gatherings, Kanban groups don't concentrate on the individual employees but instead on the work that must be finished. In Kanban, it isn't just at the daily stand-up gatherings where it is prohibited to appoint fault, it is illegal in a wide range of meetings. All together for the everyday stand-up gatherings to run as successfully and effectively as could be allowed, further or increasingly specialized conversations between singular employees are redirected into follow-up meetings. Customary meetings are frequently essentially arranged time squandering in light of the fact that a bunch of colleagues examine things with one another and 20 others are compelled to stay there and tune in despite the fact that it has nothing to do with them. This is kept away from through follow-up gatherings. The every day stand-up meeting might be the Kanban group's "own uncommon gathering," yet different partners can obviously additionally partake whenever intrigued or if the group so wants.

QUEUE REPLENISHMENT MEETING

How do the tickets get into the input queue? Through choices on the request for the work items taken in the queue replenishment meeting. This meeting happens consistently yet, can likewise be mentioned whenever wanted. These are the limits of the Kanban group's jurisdiction, and hence, those present at the replenishment meeting ought to be the following:

• All the individuals who dole out work to the group

• All the individuals who get finished work from the group

• All the individuals who can add to choices in regards to the group's next work things

Together with the group agents who give the technical aspects, internal stakeholders and representatives of outside clients likewise partake and vie for the capacities of the group. Preferably, a senior individual from the management is there as an aide to contribute regarding the whole organization's viewpoint. At last, the spots in the input queue are stipulated by as WIP limits; the choice with respect to when a work item is to be prepared should likewise be made, putting relevance of business in mind. It could happen that a change at the higher corporate level of the organization happens because of these meetings. All things considered, individuals meeting here have private information on the vital and strategic effect of different groupings of work items. Past these Kanban meetings, these individuals are all the time disengaged when working. They meet up in the queue replenishment meeting and, frequently after an underlying fight for the best spot in the input queue, look for solutions that bode well for the whole organization.

In the traditional methodology, the group gets contributions from all engaged with the progressing work process. As have already been established, in such a circumstance, everything typically has a high need since the individual wishes of colleagues aren't constantly founded on contemplations about costs of postponement. In this way, in Kanban, there's need to direct occupations in meetings, subsequently staying away from the circumstance where employees are continually hauled away from their present work items and have extra ones that could possibly be financially feasible heaped upon them, constraining them to continually switch between them. To do this, all work things are gathered in a funnel during the queue replenishment meeting including, for instance, a backlog, a ticketing framework, or a request tool, before they are then placed into the input queue. We gather the stakeholders at one table with the goal that they can together, as opposed to each for themselves, choose the order wherein work items are to be given to the group and the classes of service these work items are to be doled out. The impact is that the group orders its work items, works in harmony, and can more readily comply with its time constraints, which is in light of a legitimate concern for the partners.

What is the ideal frequency for the queue replenishment meeting? It is set up that the ideal size of the input queue relies upon the throughput of the group and the frequency of queue replenishment meetings. Then again, the frequency of the meeting relies upon the throughput of the group and the size of the input queue. A week by week meeting is suitable most times, yet we have additionally worked with groups who might get together at short notification if necessary. There is no best solution. The perfect solution is an aftereffect of trial, perception, and change.

Backlog Maintenance

With the Wip-limited input queues, classes of service, and queue replenishment meetings, control mechanism are made that ought to incite the partners to have a detailed conversation as far as what they need the group to accomplish for them. Obviously, there is impressive risk that these desires—should they succumb to economically progressively significant work items—by the by, land in the backlog and stay there, seeking after better occasions. In any case, it's entirely basic that these work items are essentially overlooked by the customers on the grounds that eventually, everything wasn't exactly so significant, all things considered. It's clearly increasingly wonderful for a development group if they don't need to go around conveying a sack loaded with such work items Also, members in the queue replenishment meeting shouldn't need to work through a heap of work items on numerous occasions so as to set up which are to be placed into the input queue at first. For productivity, the backlog should just comprise of work items that have a genuine possibility of usage. It is along these lines beneficial for the members of the queue replenishment meeting to look at the backlog intently at ordinary interims and choose which work items could be expelled. As a rule, you can set up strategies for this, for instance, "All items of backlog that haven't been taken up in a half year are to be disposed of." In incredibly dynamic situations, we have once in a while observed this deadline shortened to as meager as 2 months. Different groups have decided on a two-stage process and give the ticket holder an underlying admonition that their item is on the "to throw" list, permitting the previous customer to consider whether the ticket is as yet pertinent or not.

Despite the methodology: A little backlog makes it simpler to sort work into a processing order. If, in spite of an expectation, a work item that has been discarded should be sure to be implemented, at that point it advances once more into the backlog and is raised again at subsequent queue replenishment meetings.

RELEASE PLANNING MEETINGS

Not at all like the everyday stand-ups and queue replenishment meetings, the frequency of the release planning meetings relies upon the point in time at which a release is to happen. Kanban doesn't have any necessities for the interim between releases. The delivery interim consistently relies upon the setting wherein work is done and the quality or level of refinement of the item to be given. Notwithstanding, certain consistency in delivery is alluring for the basic explanation that it reinforces clients' trust. This is as valid for software development, in same way for public transport services. In the event that you routinely take the underground you don't take a gander at the clock since you're used to the regular time intervals between trains. In any case, if you're taking the train for a more extended journey, it's significant for your very own orientation to know when the train leaves and when it will show up since the frequency right now is not just guaranteed. The input interval of the queue replenishment meetings and the output interval of the release planning meetings needn't really be indistinguishable. In the event that a Kanban group has built up a fortnightly frequency of release, for instance, at that point, the release replenishment meetings should happen each fortnight or daily. The queue replenishment meeting can all things considered, happen week after week or even daily if the group's throughput so demands.

The release planning meeting is to be attended to by everybody required for the release or keen on the present release, for instance:

• Configuration managers and system and operations specialists

• developers, analyzers, and business experts

• direct superiors and management

Releases, by the way, even those without Kanban, work best with checklists or agendas. At first, all fundamental points are gathered in an agenda that must be finished so as to ensure a delivery that is successful. These focuses are then adjusted for the present release and the present conditions set up in the release planning meeting.

What is a good delivery Cadence?

Another inquiry should be made so as to have the option to respond to this above question: When is a delivery economical convenient? Releases don't in any case come free. Contingent upon the sort and unpredictability of a project, the expenses of delivery can make up a truly significant piece of the absolute expenses. As a rule, two sorts of delivery costs must be considered:

1. Coordination costs: contain all the exercises required for the coordination of a conveyance including the release planning meetings themselves.

2. Exchange costs: before a software can be exhibited to a client, tests must be carried out, database plans moved, servers arranged, and backups made.

So as to find out delivery proficiency, we ascertain the extent of the all-out costs the delivery costs comprise. Assume the expenses for a fortnightly delivery cadence in a project with all out expenses of €100,000 are €80,000. The efficiency of delivery is 20%, that is, 80% of the expenses are for the costs of delivery. Is this positive or negative from a monetary point of view? Just replying "yes" or "no" to this inquiry is preposterous on the grounds that maybe this is a task for which delivery is requesting or significant. Every organization should in this manner locate its own response to the subject of the most alluring efficiency level. We anyway have two potential options should it be totally important to raise the delivery productivity:

1. We deliver later. Right now, the costs of delivery as an extent of the total costs no doubt continue as before. In the event that there is an increase in the delivery cadence in the example above to a monthly basis, the delivery costs as a rate, decline and the efficiency of delivery increases, proportionately. The issue with this is the delivery productivity would be at a maximum, theoretically, if we were not to deliver by any means. What's more, economically, that is presumably not such an extraordinary thought.

2. We decrease the expenses of delivery. Numerous platforms online can bear to have different releases every day due to the fact that their conveyance costs, put obtusely, comprise just of a mouse click. Arriving at this point anyway, takes a specific measure of work. Where is the potential for savings on account of different organizations? This subsequent choice again sets direct expectations for the capacity of the framework to improve. What we can do to diminish the expenses of delivery relies on the individual circumstance.

Kanban is totally in favor of a delivery cadence. Nonetheless, it doesn't endorse which of the two ways of expanded productivity that one should make use of and what the ideal delivery cadence is. This is on the grounds that, because of the enormous contrasts in requests, it is neither conceivable nor reasonable to offer such expressions. The frequency of input and that of the output don't really need to be in a state of harmony. The most significant factor in finding the suitable cadence ought to consistently be economic practicality. This is one reason Kanban doesn't highlight iterations in predefined timeboxes (which obviously doesn't imply that you can't work with timeboxes!). Work items can't generally be conveyed so that they fit into timeboxes. One counterproductive response to this is the work items are just made to fit so they can be finished inside a timebox. Kanban isolates the prioritization of work items in the queue replenishment meeting from advancement and delivery. The delivery cadences don't need to be fixed to the prioritization cadence if they don't compare to the manner in which the team works or are not economically convenient.

TEAM RETROSPECTIVES

The aspect of retrospectives is constantly worried about evaluating work, especially work done in a collaborative manner, occurring inside a particular time period and reaching conclusions on what can be improved. They thusly investigate the manner in which the group works. Retrospectives are typically held with a defined frequency. In any case, as learned, improvement ought to happen constantly in Kanban. When an issue shows up, one contemplates how it tends to be settled and how the work process can be advanced. From this Kaizen point of view, retrospectives are manually made takeoffs from regular daily existence through which a separation that is artificial, can be made between the presence of an issue and its instructive worth. In any case, all things considered, it isn't the case that everybody is in a situation to promptly execute the concept of

Kaizen in their day by day work. Before there can be a culture of persistent improvement, you first need a culture of progress. This is one reason Kanban additionally puts accentuation on developmental change with regards to retrospectives. Retrospectives made weekly are entirely reasonable when a group starts working with Kanban. In these meetings, the group, the executives, and other included group of individuals gather proposals for enhancements and sort them in priority order. Numerous groups think that its valuable to introduce an improvements board (or upgrades backlog) so as to actualize upgrades in a steady progression. We have likewise observed groups utilize a different class of service for upgrades.

In any case, retrospectives are additionally reasonable if a Kanban group effectively utilizes Kaizen thinking. While concentrating on the present nearby optimization in a segment of the value chain, you mustn't dismiss the way that everything must occur in terms of the master plan—the whole value chain of your organization. Seen from this perspective, retrospectives are useful in light of the fact that a group can make a stride back and set up whether the requirement for all-encompassing improvements at numerous points in an organization have gotten obvious because of local upgrades. In Lean creation, Kaizen alludes to transformative, steady improvements. The idea "Kaikaku" conversely represents large, progressive, and radical upgrades. If a Kanban team has just coordinated Kaizen thinking into its regular procedures, retrospectives can become Kaikaku occasions where the acknowledgment of local improvements can be amassed into upgrades at an all-encompassing, foundational level.

OPERATIONS REVIEWS

The comprehensive view is additionally at the core of activities reviews. Each Kanban group increases significant experience during its work—experience that prompts self-improvement yet, ought to improve the whole organization. With activities surveys, we attempt to beat the discontinuity from which organizations "endure," portrayed by Eliyahu M. Goldratt. In review of activities, all the Kanban groups in an organization meet up so as to impart their experiences to one another and explain issues and connections that surpass the limits of the individual groups. The management and partners are explicitly free to attend so as to get a picture of the advancement being made and a superior inclination for where their specific aptitudes could be of administration. Preferably, tasks reviews should occur on a month to month premise and last around 2 h. Time management in a strict manner and great moderation are required. During this meeting, each group gives the estimations which they screen their work process and the ends that can be drawn from them. The review is in this manner a goal, data-driven activity for the effective performance of the organization.

CHAPTER EIGHT

KAIZEN AND KANBAN

FAILURE: BARRIERS TO

SUCCESSFUL

IMPLEMENTATION

Failing to Improve

If you ever choose to take the Kaizen way, you then have a look back and see that you are doing things the very same way you were doing them a year prior, don't have any questions—you are falling. Individuals appear to accept somewhere down in their brains that, regardless of whether we continue doing things a similar way, results will improve after some time because of training. Obviously, there is a major contrast between unimportant redundancy and conscious practice, the sort of training where you are continually attempting to discover new, better methods for getting things done.

Then again, simply changing things continually without a reasonable purpose or some pattern doesn't ensure that the progressions that are introduced are making a difference. Likewise, with self-organization, change for the sake of having a change isn't really something worth being thankful for. Change is an essential condition so as to improve, yet not all change or progressions will cause you to improve. Obviously, we should set up some improvement-related measurements—profitability, quality, or even group satisfaction. Be that as it may, never trust metrics to an extreme—use them similarly as a marker of what may be going on. The explanation not to pay attention to metrics too seriously, is on the grounds that metrics are hard—if certainly feasible—in an information-based condition. How would you measure a designer's efficiency? Is it about how long he/she works? At that point, if two designers work a similar number of hours, would they say they are similarly productive? Consider the most productive individual in your environment—how would you know it? Is there something you can really check, or is it rather something you feel?

Likewise know: what you measure is the thing that you'll get. In the event that you measure 'working hours', you'll get a lot of them—and that is not constantly something worth being thankful for, except if you can charge for them regardless of what the outcomes are and you couldn't care less about the moral ramifications of such a business. Anyway, we simply characterized the most significant approach to realize you are coming up short at Kaizen and Kanban—nothing changes. Obviously, after some time, it is pivotal that you can portray your specific, explicit wanted state and survey the differences with the present or past states.

Try not to wrongly go for the entire change too rapidly: one of the most widely recognized suggestions you'll get from Kaizen specialists is 'don't make your Kaizen scope too enormous'. Regardless of whether you have a clear image or idea of where you need to be later on, it's smarter to concur that it will require some more investment or time, than you anticipate. That way, you can concentrate your short term endeavors on the initial move toward the full usage of the ideal state.

Over all, in a long-lasting Kaizen change—and there is no other kind—you ought to have the option to think back in time and differentiate between how you were playing out a year prior and how are you performing presently, even with no unequivocal measurements. Try not to trick yourself attempting to quantify improvement after each cycle, month, or quarter—it develops, and it's hard to distinguish the tiny increments.

Reasons Why Kaizen Fails

Absence of a genuine culture.

Kaizen is considered just to be another procedure, tool, or even trend. There is no activity planned for changing individuals' practices or value framework; far more detestable: activities and practices conflicting with the Kaizen Culture are not contended back. There is no reasonable wanted state and there is no honorable motivation behind the Kaizen activity. Existing and pervasive culture and procedures will likewise forestall Kaizen, particularly if there is a culture of 'you can't contact', 'this is the manner in which we've constantly done it', or 'this isn't my/your obligation'.

Politics and blame games.

This is a particular instance of social clash: those in charge are increasingly worried about 'concealing the trash' and who is to be accused for any issue or imperfection than really captivating, in a useful discussion on the best way to improve. There is no genuine management purchase in. Some of the time it even appears as inactive forceful practices—managers will swear they are into the Kaizen change, yet then will undermine it. There is normally no straightforwardness and there is a dread of conveying and making information accessible to everybody.

General resistance to change.

Individuals simply decline to change in light of the fact that any change—particularly a major one, as in a Kaizen activity—suggests moving out of their customary range of familiarity. As a matter of course, except if there is a solid explanation (the respectable motivation behind Kaizen) individuals won't understand the need to run the additional mile or take part in the improvement procedure.

Lack of momentum.

There is one enormous improvement occasion, instructional

class, or communication campaign, yet then there is no follow up or development. Individuals are advised to improve, however then there isn't sufficient communication, zero ability to see, no vitality, no champions or success stories, no speedy successes, no inner advertising of the activity, no metrics, no procedure, no preparation, and no support.

No sense of ownership/no empowerment.

Not every person is associated with the Kaizen and Kanban initiative—maybe just some managers or some management-selected Kaizen jobs, who will be viewed as the 'people liable for Kaizen'. Individuals will feel that Kaizen is simply one more weight tossed at them. Individuals won't have the option to nitpick directors, decide, or, figuratively, stop the line. When faced with obstacles, the normal answer will be 'it's not our flaw' or 'we previously told the manager, go speak with them'. Some of the time, an indication of no genuine proprietorship and empowerment can be recognized when you see the organization making 'Kaizen circles' or 'Kaizen squads' at the levels of management as opposed to enlisting everybody into the Kaizen activity (in this way, once more, Kaizen winds up being something that the 'Kaizen people's do).

Short term vision.

Kaizen is definitely not a genuine need. The organization experiences short-sighted vision, so monetary objectives and undertaking delivery dates are viewed as more significant than Kaizen activities and their related venture. In different cases, Kaizen is viewed as a short term undertaking with an end date.

Failure to recognize problems.

Japanese Lean Sensei as a rule asked western workers what issues they had the option to spot at the line of production, and much of the time the appropriate response was 'We are doing fine here! Forget about it!'. The Sensei consistently replied back: 'No problem is a problem'. It implies that your people have lived such a great amount of time with their issues that now they are repetitive sound, like music in the background that you never again notice. A subsequent stage comes when your kin distinguish enormous obstacles yet can't partition them in littler parts that they can handle. Some of the time, a variation of this problem is that individuals neglect to prioritize their activities, and some of the time they go after significant—however hard to solve—issues as opposed to going for the 'low hanging foods grown from the ground' speedy successes to empower the improvement activity.

Inability to see root causes.

We simply apply easy routes and workarounds, yet the genuine problem causes are covered up and are rarely solved. Problems are redundant—the attention is on momentary solutions as opposed to contributing sufficient time to see all the causal relations and all the suggested factors. As the first causes are not tackled, in some cases a similar reason can traverse various issues in an eccentric manner.

Inability to plan and execute.

An ideal state is defined (plan) and afterward some activity is performed (do). Obstacles are distinguished (check). However, nothing is truly done so as to evacuate obstructions and have the system redefined (demonstration!). This sort of 'failed Deming cycle' is the thing that you see when Retrospectives end with a rundown of things we are doing well and things we are fouling up, but there is no plan of action so as to address those issues.

Lack of resources.

Not really in the feeling of physical resources: now and again there is sufficiently not time nor abilities to approach Kaizen in a beneficial manner. On numerous events, groups will be approached to improve, yet then there won't be any organized time to analyze, reflect, and plan for development, nor any time or assets to commit to the planned improvements.

Change Management

So as to change your way of life, you need to comprehend change elements. There are the absolute most significant reasons any change activity fails. Presumably, the principal reason change fails is established in the start of your change initiative. An organization that is attempting to transform, begin top-down (the executive's message to the organization), and the change was routed to everybody in the organization simultaneously.

At the point when you attempt to disclose a plan to the entire arrangement of individuals, the early dominant part will remain quiet, and the late majority will be doubters. Loafers, then again, will assault any endeavor at change, regardless of its tendency. So fundamentally, doubters and loafers will dwarf the innovators and the early adopters, and the thought will be killed.

So as to augment your odds of progress with the presentation of any thought, you need to brood it in the sheltered condition given by the early adopters. At that point, you need to give little successes and realities to the early majority to make the change look attractive and all the safer for them. You ought to tune in to cynics, as they will distinguish opposition arguments—'I don't care for this thought in light of the fact that A, B, and C'. With respect to loafers, you ought to overlook them. They seldom give levelheaded contentions, and they simply oppose change as a result of its inclination. In any case, loafers will—hesitantly—follow the greater part when it is persuaded, or they will move to some other spot where they don't need to receive the change.

The second most significant motivation behind why change comes up short is, the failure to plan and execute the change initiative. Change needs steady vitality—it's thermodynamics! Without vitality or energy, the framework will consistently haul to chaos, disorder, and the lowest effort state. There are a few different ways to continue such energy in your change initiative, however most likely the best ones depend on 'people and interactions', i.e., having individuals going about as change specialist/change evangelists. Being a change operator is hard. It implies individuals will continually overlook you or even toss stones at you—become acclimated to it! Yet, regardless of the amount you grasp being a change specialist, keep in mind how it can influence your inspiration. It is significant that change specialists make a network of training where they can share their agony and get some support. Understand that change specialists are not intended to really execute change. Their obligation, then again, is to make everybody mindful of the significance and allure of the change, to move them, and propel them. Change operators recount stories and make individuals need to partake in building a superior future.

A portion of undisputed top choices are.

– How would you intend to convey change, or make everybody mindful of the activity? How are you emanating information and facilitating communication? How are you upholding discourse and interest?

– Is there any way you are boosting the change and making it attractive? At the end of the day, how might this benefit them?

– Is there any ability individuals need so as to make the improvement occur? If that is the situation, would you say you are preparing individuals and allowing them to practice?

– How are you binding together this change to the identity of the group? Is it accurate to say that you are relating change to the group's motivation, values, objectives, practices, and needs?

– Are you mindful of the obstructions and obstacles to change? What actions are you taking to evacuate them?

– Have you tended to the standard producers looking for early adopters or even change champions?

A generally ignored explanation behind change failure is to not consider how the change is affecting everybody. Our environment and our practices decide in extraordinary part, what our identity is, the possibility of self we produce after some time. Along these lines, the emotional pieces of our brains think about any endeavor to change our environment or practices as an endeavor to change our selves—hence, it is viewed as an animosity. In other words, our thinking is hard-wired to respond forcefully and adversely to change, particularly if it originates from an external source.

Some of the time we are so amped up for our own thoughts for change and improvement that we neglect to perceive how this change influences others' thoughts of security, status, power, impact, solace, or information. Another procedure can be an incredible improvement for the organization, yet it can likewise undermine individuals' certainty on their own abilities, and they may respond contrarily to it. That doesn't mean they need to be promptly marked as 'loafers' or 'not cooperative individuals'; there may be a legitimate individual purpose behind change avoidance, regardless of whether we neglect to see that reason or regardless of whether they don't know about their very own motivations to oppose change.

At last, one of the more straightforward reasons change fails is on the grounds that individuals don't continue the exertion sufficiently long to get change going. There's a fantasy about 'medium-term achievement's and it is only that—a myth. In the event that you study probably the most-referenced instances of medium-term achievement otherwise known as "overnight success", you will find that there was a great deal of work and continued exertion behind it.

Things to do

Essentially, you should acknowledge and befriend the possibility that you (perusing this book) should review all these Kaizen issues and change obstacles so as to simply get things moving. As a little instruction of what you will do is:

> You have to persuade everybody that Kaizen is, for fact, a culture and not a procedure, tool, or structure. You have to

accumulate all the trend-setters and early adopters and begin chipping away at a mutual reason and common values. You have to begin gathering anecdotes about change, tales about the future, stories that individuals can advise to one another. Recollect that accounts are all over: clients, suppliers, workers, managers, partners, and communities. It's not necessary that these accounts talk about your organization toward the start—you can recount tales about Toyota or any organization individuals appreciate; the thought is to give them an ideal social state to find a workable pace. You will begin giving acknowledgment and encouraging feedback on everything that is lined up with the social express that you defined through purpose and value—discover them accomplishing something right! You ought to likewise begin spreading Kaizen ancient rarities—A3 Problem Solving diagrams, Visual Kaizen Boards, and Standards.

You will begin to convey the message that we are all ready in the Kaizen process, and will stop any blame games when discussing problems. You will make cross-practical improvement groups and will look for paranoid fear of the management or absence of interest. You will have one-on-one instructing meetings both with individuals attempting to follow up on their own, managers manhandling their powers, and individuals lingering behind. You will uphold straightforwardness and the utilization of visual management.

You will plan and keep up a consistent change management project. To do that, you will find out about change and continually survey the change management systems, updating and adjusting them to the present reality of the organization culture. You will urge individuals to escape their usual ranges of familiarity and celebrate learning (through both failures and achievement). You will continually remind everybody about the basic reason, the ideal express, the respectable purpose that we are seeking after.

You will continually infuse energy into the Kaizen and Kanban procedure. You will mind that everyone watches the Kaizen occasions and that there is sufficient organized and secured time for learning, research, advancement, and self-improvement. You will make and support more Kaizen evangelists, specialists, champions, and leaders. You will continue and support Kaizen and Kanban people group. You will give individuals training, backing, literature, and mentorship. You will impart and commend all upgrades. You will mind to set up the sufficient improvement metrics and make them noticeable and essential to all.

You will ensure that everybody is remembered for the Kaizen and Kanban plan. You will encourage dynamic assignment of expert on creation groups. In order to do such, you will recognize key choice regions and define the present degree of appointment. You will mentor groups so as to make them increasingly develop and, thus, capable of being in authority. You will develop duty and responsibility, first through a culture of trust, straightforwardness, and nonappearance of fault, and afterward by requesting duty and development. You will bolster groups when they progress and develop in duty, and ensure they utilize their strengthening by setting sufficient settings and arrangement with corporate objectives. You will forestall relapses when a group commits errors: you will work with both group and supervisors to ensure they gain from their mix-ups and keep comparable slip-ups from occurring later on.

CHAPTER NINE

PITFALLS TO AVOID

At this point you ought to have a lot of motivations to utilize Kaizen and Kanban in your process. You can show interested individuals that it has improved and keeps on improving your process. Due to the methodology that Kaizen and Kanban takes to change the management ("Start where you are and improve from that point"), most groups and organizations don't protest loudly to Kaizen and Kanban and the standards it's based on. All things considered, some analysis comes up every now and then. It wouldn't be reasonable in the event that we didn't at any rate address the most well-known issues and how to manage them. Generally, the criticisms centers around entanglements or pitfalls that are anything but difficult to fall into if you don't watch out. We composed this part so you recognize what to keep away from. The point of this section is twofold: to acquaint you with some usually brought up criticisms and afterward to assist you with dodging the pitfalls recognized by this criticism. Finding out about the manners in which individuals criticize is an incredible method to improve—it helps ensure you avoid terrible things.

Here are a few pitfalls that you may experience and solutions that can be applied:

Pitfall: Kanban can wind up getting exhausting, with simply work item after work item arranged, and no common interruptions, festivities, or cadences.

> Solution: Compared to other methodologies, for example, Scrum, Kanban gives you the opportunity to separate the various services, for example, arranging, audit, and review, from one another, depending on how the work really courses through your process.

> Kanban is extremely lightweight and is anything but difficult to get up and running. As we've referenced a great deal, it's only a couple of straightforward standards. In case you're putting into practice other strategies, or some other emphasis based strategy, you can even evacuate stuff like iterations, if you need. In a little while, you end up with only a consistent progression of work and "no leeway ... to rest and be innovative."

> In any case, that is not how it should be, and it's not how Kanban was proposed to be. An incredible inverse! Kanban never said to expel iterations. Yet, it gives you the opportunity to segregate the services of different strategies, for example, arranging, audits, and reviews—from one another. Kanban doesn't utter a word about having a similar rhythm for various services or not. If you see that as something valuable, by all methods feel free to do that, yet don't be superfluously obliged by it. Accept the opportunity to defer choices until the "last capable minute," when you

have the most information in your grasp. Utilizing Kaizen and Kanban, you can likewise enormously profit by showcasing your partners what you've done and how you're advancing, with exhibitions and audits.

Creating cadences for celebration

To battle the hazard that your process is simply "work, work, work," you could and ought to have a cadence for celebration. It's as significant as different occasions that have been discussed, and it's an extraordinary method to help boost morale and group satisfaction. Cadences for celebration can take numerous structures, and there's regularly no deficiency of imagination with regards to designing better approaches to celebrate.

The use of Frequent flyer miles can be used as a way of having celebration cadences as a major aspect of your procedure includes;

Frequent flyer miles

With this, the group can gather points for the work they're doing. They would then be able to utilize such points to accomplish something fun together. The points work a lot of like a carrier's preferred flyer miles—after you travel a specific number of miles, the aircraft gives you a few points to spend on free excursions, upgraded hotel lodgings, or different advantages. The group and the partner concoct some approach to follow the focuses earned by the group and choose what to do when the group arrives at a specific point threshold. For instance, when you've finished 50 story points or 20 work items, you have a pizza and gaming evening at the workplace.

Pitfall: Kanban has no worked in time boxing. You need time boxes on the grounds that they assist you with organizing and make vital exchange offs in scope, time, and cost.

Solution: You can have time boxes where they're valuable. In flow-based procedures, without emphasis, time boxing can be executed with SLAs and deadlines per work item, for instance. Time boxing is a ground-breaking method that encourages you keep up center and settle on the fundamental choices to convey the correct things on schedule. The triangle is one approach to show what time boxing is about. It delineates the trade-offs you need to make in any project, yet specifically for programming projects (in some cases called the iron triangle or triple requirements).

This triangle adjusts scope, time, and cost against one another. Scope alludes to the extent of the features somebody needs. Cost is how a lot of cash it will cost—for instance, what number of individuals are in the group and which software/hardware is expected to have it built, and different expenses. Time speaks to what extent the undertaking will take, or the due date when the task should be finished. In the triangle is a fourth perspective: quality. You can mull over quality and make tradeoffs with it. As a general rule, that creates issues thereafter in the form of technical debts that should be paid off. We don't regularly prescribe exchanging with quality but rather propose attempting to make the quality very good, considering different perspectives.

Pitfall: Kanban adopts a transformative strategy to change the management and urges you to begin where you are, consent to seek after gradual change, and regard current processes and jobs. However, imagine a scenario in which you need a resolution. Consider the possibility that the organization or the group should be shaken and mixed a piece.

Solution: You're in charge of the pace at which you need to improve. Utilize a lower WIP limit to incite greater improvement opportunities, for instance. Or on the other hand, begin utilizing new practices, for example, test-driven development (TDD) and pair programing at a pace that is appropriate for your organization. Kanban is extraordinary on the grounds that it begins where you are. You can start utilizing Kanban without changing a thing. Just picture the manner in which you work and breaking point the quantity of things going on simultaneously. From that, you can improve and develop your procedure as you find out more.

This is uplifting news since it implies you effectively can bring Kanban into practically any condition, paying little heed to the procedure you're working with today. There's no enormous detonation, no changing of titles and jobs—you can continue functioning as you used to. The representation part is something that even the most enthusiastic adversaries of better approaches for working can regularly live with, as long as you keep it lined up with the manners in which you work now.

To put it plainly, Kanban can be presented as an advancement, maintaining a strategic distance from difficult revolutionary changes. At this point, you may consider how on Earth this can be a Kanban criticism. It's anything but difficult to see, in fact: for reasons unknown, you need a transformation. Now and then you have to shake things up and get your organization to wake up. So as to endure or make the most of new business opportunities, you may need to change a ton, and change quick. If that is the situation, at that point you ought to most likely go with a strategy that is tried and tested (like Scrum or XP) and afterward include the Kaizen and Kanban standards to drive improvement. You can consider it as far as risk appraisal: a little, pliable group, with an ability to have a go at something new and an incredible mentor close by, can presumably take a ton of progress without gambling excessively. Then again, in case you're a Cobol group in a major, traditionalist bank organization, the danger of changing is more noteworthy.

Pitfall: Because it's only three straightforward standards, Kanban doesn't direct much by any stretch of the imagination. This can in some cases, become a reason to quit doing things that are helping you today. You may get apathetic.

Solution: Keep doing the practices you have discovered valuable until you see a valid justification to quit utilizing them. At the point when they frustrate your flow, at that point you can begin addressing how or whether you ought to do planning, assessing, emphases, etc. A few groups that start "doing" Kanban quit doing the great practices that some other strategy has given them, for example, standups, reviews, and surveys. We regularly hear stuff like "We used to design our work, however now, with Kanban, we've halted that." Other groups are the inverse and don't start with Agile practices in any case. "Scrum doesn't work for us! We attempted an arranging meeting yesterday, and it was exhausting. Rather we'll do the new thing called Kanban. It's just a stand up (we may expel it later) and some stickie on a divider. That is sufficient for us."

Until you discover valid justification to stop, continue doing the following: reviews, audits, and sprints (with a session of planning towards the start and a survey toward the end). Continue composing long specifications archives and giving them over in the following stage in your procedure.

Kanban will before long give you what's hindering your flow. On your visualized work process (on the board, for instance), you can see when work things are piling up. Your measurements and outlines may enable you to see where the procedure is eased back down. These things may in the end lead you to begin scrutinizing the manner in which you compose details or specifications, handoffs, etc.

Some of the many things that we've seen numerous Kanban groups run into isn't utilizing WIP limits. You'd feel that most groups would consider that (since it's one of just three standards), however it happens a great deal. Here's an exceptionally basic situation that numerous groups end up with while bringing Kaizen and Kanban into their procedure: A ton of groups begin utilizing Kanban standards with no WIP limits. This is a slip-up, as we would like to think. With no WIP limits, there's no strain to drive you to improve your procedure. You can simply continue including work in process when issues emerge. Regularly this shows as a great deal of blocked or holding up work items on the board. You can compare this to a cycle that can be broadened uncertainly. There's no motivator to finish the extension for the cycle on schedule—you can generally expand the degree. Recollect the genuine idea of a WIP limit: it is anything but a standard, however a rule and a conversation trigger. Without it, there's no motivation to have the conversation. You simply continue adding work to your procedure, and there's no instrument to ask whether you ought to do this or not.

Lightning Source UK Ltd.
Milton Keynes UK
UKHW022011310822
408147UK00003B/340